Bible Study for
Young Adults
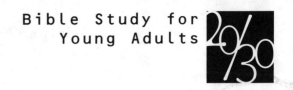

LOVE

Opening Your Heart to God and Others

Barbara K. Mittman

D1403390

Abingdon Press
Nashville

Love: Opening Your Heart to God and Others

by Barbara K. Mittman

Copyright © 2000 by Abingdon Press

ISBN 0-687-07316-2

This book is printed on acid-free paper.

MANUFACTURED IN THE UNITED STATES OF AMERICA.

04 05 06 07 08 09—10 9 8 7 6 5 4 3

CONTENTS

MEET THE WRITER

Barbara K. Mittman is an ordained deacon, certified in Christian education and youth ministry. She currently serves as the Iowa Conference Youth Coordinator and with First United Methodist Church in Nevada, Iowa. Barb has previously published church school curriculum for youth and is the author of *Exodus: Leaving Behind Moving On* in this 20/30 series.

WELCOME TO 20/30: BIBLE STUDY FOR YOUNG ADULTS

The *20/30* Bible study series is offered for post-modern adults who want to participate in and help structure their own discoveries—in life, in relationships, in faith. In each of the volumes of this series, we will have the opportunity to use our own experience in life and faith to examine the biblical texts in new ways. We will examine biblical images that shape all of our lives, even if we are not immediately aware that they do.

Image Is Everything

Images are what shape our decisions. We may think or know certain important data that weigh heavily in a decision. We may value the advice and counsel of others. We may find that the stated or implied wishes of others influence what we do. But in the end, it is often the *image* we hold that makes the decision.

For example, perhaps you were deeply hurt by someone important to you— an employer, a friend, even a pastor. You know in your heart that the institution is not to blame or that friendships are based on more than one event. But the image shaped by the difficult experience is that the job, or the friend, or the church cannot be relied upon. You *know* better, but you just have to make a change anyway. The image was more powerful than the reason.

Images are powerful, and they are familiar. In each of the studies in this series, you will encounter a well-known image that will connect your familiar experiences with some basis in Scripture.

You love and are loved in return, and you know this is more than just a matter of emotion. *Love: Opening Your Heart to God and Others* will guide you into the biblical understanding of love and help you explore many facets of love, and love gone wrong, with God, family, friends, and life partner.

You define for yourself what you think is "the good life." Is your definition complete? *Abundance: Living Responsibly With God's Gifts* will guide you into the biblical understanding of abundant life and help you sort out many of the faithful and practical issues that come together in a life of abundance.

You know how important it is to have a sense of support and roots; to have friends and a life partner. *Community: Living Faithfully With Others* introduces you to Scriptures and life examples that delve into intimacy, work, and family relationships, and more.

You have faith, but may also realize that it can mean many things. Is it belief or trust, or waiting or moral behavior, or something else? Or is it all those things? *Faith: Living a Spiritual Life* helps you examine your faith and grow as a Christian.

You know what it's like to make agreements, to establish commitments, to give your word and expect to be trusted. *Covenant: Making Commitments That Count* engages you in study sessions that explain a variety of covenants, what happens when covenants are broken, how to have a faithful covenant to care for others and for the earth, and certainly, what it means to have this sacred covenant with God.

You know what it is like to move to a new place, to have to deal with transitions in school or work or in relationships. You have probably experienced changes in your family as you have grown up and moved out on your own. Some of these moves are gradual, just taken in stride. Others can be painful or abrupt; certainly life-changing. In *Exodus: Leaving Behind, Moving On*, you will appreciate learning how God is in the midst of those movements, no matter how minor or how transformational.

Experience, Faith, Growth, and Action

Each volume in this series will help you probe, on your own terms, how your experience links with your faith and how deepening your faith develops your life experience. If you need a prompt for your reflection, each volume has several pages of real life case studies. As your faith and commitment to Jesus Christ grow, you may be looking for ways to be involved in specific service opportunities. Several are listed on pages 79-80.

We hope this series will help you encounter God through Scripture, reflection, and dialogue with others who desire to grow in faith, and to serve others. One image we hold is that God is in all things. God is certainly with you.

HOW TO USE THIS RESOURCE

Each session of this resource includes similar components or elements:
- A statement of the issue or question to be explored
- Several "voices" of persons who are currently dealing with that issue
- Exploration of biblical passages relative to the question raised
- "Bible 101" boxes that provide insight about the study of the Bible
- Questions for reflection and discussion
- Suggested individual and group activities designed to bring the session to life
- Optional case studies (found in the back of the book)
- Various service learning activities related to the session (found in the back of the book)

Choices, Choices, Choices

Collectively, these components mean one thing: *choice.* You have choices to make concerning how to use each session of this resource. Want just the nitty-gritty Bible reading, reflection, and study for personal or group use? Then focus your attention on just those components during your study time.

Like starting with real-life stories about issues then moving into how the Bible might be relevant? Start with the "voices" and move on from there. Use the "voices" to encourage group members to speak about their own experiences.

Prefer highly charged discussion encounters where many different viewpoints can be heard? Start the session with the biblical passages, followed by the questions and group activities. Be sure to compare the ideas found in the "Bible 101" boxes with your current ideas for more discussion. Want the major challenge of applying biblical principles to a difficult problem? After reading the biblical material, read one of the case studies, using the guideline provided on page 14 or get involved with one of the service learning components, described on pages 79-80.

Great Versatility

This resource has been designed for many different uses. Some persons will use this resource for personal study and reflection. Others will want to explore the work with a small group of friends. And still other folks will see this book as a different type of Sunday school resource.

Spend some time thinking about your own questions, study habits, and learning styles or those of your small group. Then use the guidelines mentioned above to fashion each session into a unique Bible study session to meet those requirements.

Highly Participatory

As you will see, the Scriptures, "voices," commentary, and experience of group members will provide an opportunity for an active, engaging time together. The greatest challenge for a group leader might be "crowd control"—being sure everyone has the chance to put his or her ideas into the mix!

The Scriptures will help you and those who study with you to make connections between real life issues and the Bible. This resource values and encourages personal participation as a means to fully understand and appreciate the intersection of personal belief with God's ongoing work in each and every life.

ON ORGANIZING A SMALL GROUP

Learning with a small group of persons offers certain advantages over studying by yourself. First, you will hopefully encounter different opinions and ideas, making the experience of Bible study a richer and more challenging event. Second, any leadership responsibilities can be shared among group members. Third, different persons will bring different talents. Some will be deep thinkers while other group members will be creative giants. Some persons will be newcomers to the Bible; their questions and comments will help others clarify their deeply held assumptions.

So how does one go about forming a small group? Follow the steps below and see how easy this task can be.

- **Read through the resource carefully.** Think about the ideas presented, the questions raised, and the exercises suggested. If the sessions of this work excite you, it will be easier for you to spread your enthusiasm to others.

- **Spend some time thinking about church members, friends, and coworkers who might find the sessions of this resource interesting**. On a sheet of paper, list two characteristics or talents you see in each person that would make him or her an attractive Bible study group member. Some talents might include "deep thinker," "creative wizard," or "committed Christian." Remember: the best small group has members who differ in learning styles, talents, ideas, and convictions, but who respect the dignity and integrity of the other members.

- **Most functional small groups have seven to fifteen members.** Make a list of potential group members that doubles your target number. For instance, if you would like a small group of seven to ten members, be prepared to invite fourteen to twenty persons.

- **Once your list of potential candidates is complete, decide on a tentative location and time.** Of course, the details can be negotiated with those persons who accept the invitation, but you need to sound definitive and clear to perspective group members. "We will initially set Wednesday night from 7 to 9 P.M. at my house for our meeting time" will sound more attractive than "Well, I don't know either when or where we would be meeting, but I hope you will consider joining us."

- **Make initial contact with prospective group members short, sweet, and to the point.** Say something like, "We are putting together a Bible study using a different kind of resource. When would be a good time to show you the resource and talk about the study?" Establishing a special time to make the invitation takes the pressure off the prospective group member to make a quick decision.

- **Show up at the decided time and place.** Talk with each prospective member individually. Bring a copy of the resource with you. Show each person what excites you about the study and mention the two unique characteristics or talents you feel he or she would offer the group. Tell each person the initial meeting time and location and how many weeks the small group will meet. Also mention that the need for a new time or location could be discussed during the first group meeting. Ask for a commitment to come to the first session. Thank individuals for their time.

- **Give a quick phone call or e-mail to thank all persons for their consideration and interest.** Remind persons of the time and location of the first meeting.

- **Be organized.** Use the first group meeting to get acquainted. Briefly describe the seven sessions. Have a book for each group member, and discuss sharing responsibilities for leadership.

LEADING AND
SHARING LEADERSHIP

So the responsibility to lead the group has fallen upon you? Don't sweat it. Follow these simple suggestions and you will razzle and dazzle the group with your expertise.

- **Read the session carefully.** Look up all the Bible passages. Take careful notes about the ideas, statements, questions, and activities in the session. Try all the activities.

- **Using twenty to twenty-five blank index cards, write one idea, activity, Bible passage, or question from the session on each card** until you either run out of material or cards. Be sure to look at the case studies and service learning options.

- **Spend a few moments thinking about the members of your group.** How many like to think about ideas, concepts, or problems? How many need to "feel into" an idea by storytelling, worship, prayer, or group activities? Who are the "actors" who prefer a hands-on or participatory approach, such as an art project or simulation, to grasp an idea? List the names of all group members, and record whether you believe each to be a THINKER, FEELER, or ACTOR.

- **Place all the index cards in front of you in the order in which they originally appeared in the session.** Looking at that order, ask yourself: 1) Where is the "head" of the session—the key ideas or concepts? 2) Where is the "heart" of the session in which persons will have a deep feeling response? 3) Where are the "feet"—those activities that ask the group to put the ideas and feelings to use? Separate the cards into three stacks: HEAD, HEART, and FEET.

- **Now construct the "body" for your class.** Shift the cards around, using a balance of HEAD, HEART, and FEET cards to determine which activities you will do and in what order. This will be your group's unique lesson plan. Try to choose as many cards as you have group members. Then, match the cards: HEAD and THINKERS; HEART and FEELERS; FEET and ACTORS for each member of the group. Don't forget a card for yourself. For instance, if your group has ten members, you should have about ten cards.

■ **Develop the leadership plan.** Invite these group members prior to the session to assist in the leadership. Show them the unique lesson plan you developed. Ask for their assistance in developing and/or leading each segment of the session as well as a cool introduction and a closing ritual or worship experience.

Your lesson plan should start with welcoming the participants. Hopefully everyone will have read the session ahead of time. Then, begin to move through the activity cards in the order of your unique session plan, sharing the leadership as you have agreed.

You may have chosen to have all the HEAD activities together, followed by the HEART cards. This would introduce the session's content, followed by helping group members "feel into" the issue through interactive stories, questions, and exercises with all group members. Feel free to add more storytelling, discussion, prayer, meditation, or worship.

You may next have chosen to use the FEET cards to end the session. Ask the group, "What difference should this session make in our daily lives?" You or the ACTORS should introduce the FEET cards as possible ways to discern a response. Ensuring that group members leave with a few practical suggestions for doing something different during the week is the point of this section of the unique lesson plan.

■ **Remember: Leading the group does not mean "Do it all yourself."** With a little planning, you can enlist the talents of many group members. By inviting group members to lead parts of the session that feel comfortable for them you will model and encourage shared leadership. Welcome their interests in music, prayer, worship, Bible, and so on, to develop innovative and creative Bible study sessions that can transform lives in the name of Jesus Christ.

CHOOSING TEACHING OPTIONS

This young adult series was designed, written, and produced out of an understanding of the attributes, concerns, joys, and faith issues of young adults. With great care and integrity, this image-based print resource was developed to connect biblical events and relationships with contemporary, real life situations of young adults. Its pages will promote Christian relationships and community, support new biblical learning, encourage spiritual development, and empower faithful decision-making and action.

This study is well-suited to young adults and may be used confidently and effectively. But with the great diversity within the young adult population, not every line of this study will be written "just for you." To be most relevant, some portions of the study material need to be tailored to fit your particular group. Adjustments for a good fit involve making choices from options offered by the resource. This customizing may be done easily by a designated leader who is familiar with the layout of the resource and the young adults who are using it.

What to Expect

In this study Scripture and real life images mesh together to provoke a personal response. Young adults will find themselves thinking, feeling, imagining, questioning, making decisions, professing faith, building connections, inviting discipleship, taking action, and making a difference. Scripture is at the core of each session. Scenarios weave in the dimensions of real life. Narrative and text boxes frame plenty of teaching options to offer young adults.

Each session is part of a cohesive volume, but is designed to stand alone. One session is not dependent on knowledge or experience accumulated from other sessions. A group leader can freely choose from the teaching options in an individual session without wondering about how it might affect the other sessions.

A Good Fit

For a better fit, alter the session based on what is known about the young adult participants. Young adults are a diverse constituency with varied experiences, interests, needs, and values. There is really no single defining characteristic that links young adults. Specific information about the age, employment status, household, personal relationships, and lifestyle among participants will equip a leader to make choices that ensure a good fit.

■ **Customize.** Read through the session. Notice how scenarios and teaching options move from integrating Scripture and real life dimensions to inviting a response.

■ **Look at the scenario(s).** How real is the presentation of real life? Say that the main character is a professional, white male, married, in his late twenties, and caught in a workplace dilemma that entangles his immediate superior and a subordinate from his division. Perhaps your group members are mostly college students and recent graduates, unmarried, and still on the way to being "settled." There are many differences between the man in the scenario and these group members.

As a leader, you could choose to eliminate the case study, substitute it with another scenario (there are several more choices on pages 76-79), claim the validity of the dilemma and shift the spotlight from the main character to the subordinate, or modify the description of the main character. Break-out groups based on age or employment experience might also be used to accommodate the differences and offer a better fit.

■ **Look at the teaching options.** How are the activities propelling participants toward a personal response? Perhaps the Scripture study requires more meditative quiet than is possible and a more academic, verbal, or artistic approach would offer a better fit. Maybe more direct decisions or actions would fit better than more passive or logical means. Try to keep a balance, though, that allows participants to "get out of their head" to reflect and also to move toward action.

Conceivably, there could just be too much in any one session. As a leader, you can pick and choose among teaching options, substitute case studies, take two meetings to do one session, and adapt any process to make a better fit. The tailoring process can be evaluated as adjustments are made. Judge the fit every time you meet. Ask questions that gauge relevance, and assess how the resource has stretched minds, encouraged discipleship, and changed lives.

USING BREAK-OUT GROUPS

20/30 break-out groups are small groups that encourage the personal sharing of lives and the gospel. The name "break-out" is a sweeping term that includes a variety of small group settings. A break-out group may resemble a Bible study group, an interest group, a sharing group, or other types of Christian fellowship groups.

Break-out groups offer young adults a chance to belong and personally relate to one another. Members are known, nurtured, and heard by others. Young adults may agree and disagree while maximizing the exchange of ideas, information, or options. They might explore, confront, and resolve personal issues and feelings with empathy and support. Participants can challenge and hold each other accountable to a personalized faith and stretch its links to real life and service.

Forming Break-Out Groups

The nature of these small break-out groups will depend on the context and design of the specific session. On occasion the total group of participants will be divided for a particular activity. Break-out groups will differ from one session to the next. Variations may involve the size of the group, how group members are divided, or the task of the group. Break-out groups may also be used to accommodate differences and help tailor the session plan for a better fit. In some sessions, specific group assembly instructions will be provided. For other sessions, decisions regarding the size or division of small groups will be made by the designated leader. Break-out groups may be in the form of pairs or trios, family-sized groups of three to six members, or groups of up to ten members.

They may be arranged simply by grouping persons seated next to one another or in more intentional ways by common interests, characteristics, or life experience. Consider creating break-out groups according to age; gender; type of household, living arrangements, or love relationships; vocation, occupation, career, or employment status; common or built-in connections; lifestyle; values or perspective; or personal interests or traits.

Membership

The membership of break-out groups will vary from session-to-session, or even within specific sessions. Young adults need to work at knowing and being known, so that there can be a balance between break-out groups that are more similar and those that reflect greater diversity. There may be times when more honest communication, trust, or accountability may be desired and group leaders will need to be free to self-select members for small groups.

It is important for 20/30 break-out groups to practice acceptance and to value the worth of others. The potential for small groups to encourage personal sharing and significant relationships is enhanced when members agree to exercise active listening skills, keep confidences, expect authenticity, foster trust, and develop ways of loving one another. All group members contribute to the development and function of break-out groups. Designated leaders especially need to model manners of hospitality and help ensure that each group member is respected.

Invitational Listening

Consider establishing an "invitational listening" routine that validates the perspective and affirms the voice of each group member. After a question or statement is posed, pause and allow time to think—not all persons think on their feet or talk out loud to think. Then, initiate conversation by inviting one group member, by name, to talk. This person may either choose to talk or to "pass." Either way, this person is honored and is offered an opportunity to speak and be heard. This person carries on the ritual by inviting another group member, by name, to speak. The process continues until all have been invited, by name, to talk. As each one invites another, the responsibility of acceptance and hospitality in the break-out groups is shared among all its members.

Study group members break-out to belong, to share the gospel, to care, and to watch over one another in Christian love. "So deeply do we care for you that we are determined to share with you not only the gospel of God but also our own selves, because you have become very dear to us" (1 Thessalonians 2:8).

LOVE:
OPENING YOUR HEART TO GOD AND OTHERS

Love is at the center of Christian life. We humans are created for and called to love. Love is life's starting point, its goal, and everything in between. Human fulfillment is celebrated in a life of love. God's steadfast and everlasting love empowers and gives meaning to all human love. It is the love in which all human experiences are anchored. We spend our entire lives growing in love.

Life Lived in Terms of the Great Commandment

Jesus established love as the foundation of the Christian faith and life. Each of the Synoptic Gospels offer an account of Jesus' response to the question: "Which is the most important of all the commandments?" The answer (Matthew 22:34-40; Mark 12:28-34; Luke 10:25-28) sums up the basic qualities of Christian loving and every imaginable connection. Love includes all that God created—ourselves, and all those with whom we share our world.

We are called to love God. This love is a grateful response of our whole selves to God's *hesed*—God's loving-kindness. We love self in the same way that God loves. As we grow in our capacity to freely offer and accept love for ourselves, we are better able to love our neighbors. We love our neighbor the same way we love ourselves. The love of neighbor cares for the day-to-day welfare of others in a far wider circle than affection alone can support. Love acts on behalf of our own well-being and that of friends and family, neighbors we cannot call by name, and through our most intimate relationships.

An Image of Love

Dorotheos of Gaza, a sixth century monk, offers a visual representation of the interdependent nature of abiding love. "Get a compass, ruler, and pencil. Take the compass and draw a circle. Mark the center point with the pencil. Use the ruler to draw straight lines (radii) from the center point to any number of points on the circumference of the circle. Put your finger at one point on the circumference of the circle. Trace the straight line from the point on the circle towards the center point. What happens to the relationship with the other radii as your finger gets closer to the center?"

Dorotheos suggests that the circle is the world. God is the center point, and the straight lines are the lives of human beings. The closer we are to God, the closer we get to one another. The closer we are to one another, the closer we get to God. Where do you see yourself along your life's line? Closer to the world or closer to God? To grow in love is to grow closer to God.

How We Love

Love is a goal. If we believe that God's love is infinite and boundless, then how can we possibly get to the extremes of human love? We have a whole lifetime to grow in love. By God's grace, we keep moving toward God and closer to one another.

There are qualities of human love that we can see in God—character traits that can be mirrored, nurtured, and grown. The treasure chest of love holds the capacity for loyal sacrifice, the desire to nurture and heal, and the actions of hospitality. There are enemies of love, too, such as selfishness, greed, jealousy, and betrayal. These all too human qualities threaten to close our hearts and lock-up the treasures of love.

We can't will ourselves to love. God gifts us with the ability to recognize love and the freedom to choose love. How we love shapes our decision-making and cultivates our attitudes, habits, and actions. Love is real. It is in relationship, day-in-and-day-out, with real people in real ways.

Grow in Love

We talk about being chosen and beloved by God and being called to love. These pages will help you grow in love and prompt you to act in love. Count on journal entries and real-life case studies to meet God and others. Plan to share and collect wisdom. Look for a new take on the Scriptures. Anticipate the chance to grow spiritually—to pray, journal, witness, and serve. Take advantage of ways to be accountable as you grow toward God and others. Expect to be changed!

Take your place in the world at a point on the circumference of the circle. Watch as you move toward God and others as you grow in love.

GOD'S SURE LOVE

This session will characterize the loyal, sacrificial, nurturing, and healing love of God.

GETTING STARTED

Stefany: It is so unbelievable.... The Scriptures say that God has known me since before I was known to my own mother and yet, God still loves me.

Joel: I can believe it as long as I remember that God loves me in spite of me.

Markus: In spite? You mean God holds a grudge, maybe even hates, but is still somehow obligated or forced to love?

Julia: You make God sound like somebody's doormat. Smile and love while getting stepped on all the time. God's love is loyal. I can't prove it or earn it, but I still believe it's always there.

Stefany: "Loving in spite" sounds more like something I would do. I guess I believe that God's love is supposed to be something more awesome, more incomprehensible than how I might love.

Make introductions. Get acquainted by providing each other with personal and identifying information, such as age, significant relationships, employment status, and leisure interests.

What do you believe about God's love? Join in this conversation and talk about what you believe.

GOD'S HESED

God loves. God loves us. God loves the very people we are. God loves us without qualification. Our sin cannot destroy or even dissuade God's love. God's love is steadfast in the face of judgment. Whether we can sense it or not, God's love is always there. God's love is loyal, even when we are not. *Hesed* is an attribute of God that is expressed in the action of God.

Biblical Studies 101: *Hesed*

The word *hesed* (chesed) is found in the context of the covenantal relationship with God and the people Israel. God's faithful action on behalf of the Israelites, even as they broke the covenant and turned away, is recorded throughout the Old Testament. The Hebrew *hesed* is translated as "steadfast love," "faithfulness," and "loyalty" in the Pentateuch (Exodus 34:6-7 and Dueteronomy 7:6-7), the Psalms (Psalm 36:5-10; Psalm 89:1-18) and the prophets (Isaiah 54:9-10; Jeremiah 9:23-24; 31).

Look Closer

Reading from a variety of Scripture versions, translations, paraphrases, and companion texts can often help shed some light on specific biblical texts or images. There is one companion text that particularly illuminates the loving action of God as praised and prayed in the Psalms. Consider partnering the book *Psalms for Praying: An Invitation to Wholeness*, by Nan C. Merrill, with your favorite Bible as you read from the Psalms.

Praying Psalm 103: A Journal Entry

OK God, let's talk! You may love, but I feel stuck. You may forgive, but I can't. What good does it do to belong to you if I can't face you? What good does it do for you to love if I would just as soon run the other way?

What does it mean to heal? I have my ideas, but my healing rests in you. Does healing lead to being able to love again? to know a right relationship with you? Right now that sounds so impossible!

I know your love doesn't wait. So. . . here I am God. Hold me, heal me, and crown me with your steadfast love. Let me bless your name. Amen.

GOD'S LOVE

A more thorough understanding of *hesed* reveals the character of God's love for humanity. It is that unwavering, responsive, everlasting, determined, and unshakable loving-kindness that is lived out in God's covenant with Israel. It is the persistent wooing of God—a love that just can't let go. *Hesed* describes an intimate, tender, and vulnerable love that does not depend on "being good." It is characterized by loyalty, sacrifice, nurturing, and the healing of those who cry out in trouble.

BIBLE

Praying Psalm 103
Meet God in Psalm 103. Read the psalm once or twice—slowly, softly, out loud, or silently moving your lips. From memory write down the words or phrases that stay with you. Think about those words and phrases. What do they mean? What, do you think, was the psalmist feeling? What do these words and phrases mean to you—your history, your life, your world? Gather your thoughts. Pick up your journal or sit with a trusted friend. Turn to God and speak to God in the first-person (God as "You"). Tell God what you thought and felt. What did you find out about God's *hesed*?

SMALL GROUP

God's Love
The prophet Hosea presents human and relational metaphors to portray God's redeeming love. If the text and its relationships are accepted as autobiographical, then it can be said that Hosea explains God's loyal and unconditional love by example.

Look to the Hosea texts to characterize God's sure love. Use the questions provided with each characterization (loyal, sacrificial, nurturing, healing) to start discussion. You may choose to spend time with the Scripture independently, in pairs, or in break-out groups. Either explore all the texts, choose just one of the characteristics of God's *hesed*, or divide the texts among break-out groups.

Loyal Love
Read Hosea 1:1-3 and
2:1-23. Use a Bible
commentary to understand it
more fully. Hosea's loyal love
would not let Gomer go. He
endured her whoring and made
plans to have her back. How radical is this husband's love? What
tactics did Hosea use to get
Gomer back? What promises
were made to make this love a
reality? What does this tell you
about the love of God for persons? for Israel or any other
group? for persons in intimate
relationships?

What song titles or
lyrics can you think of
that summarize the
symbolic actions of Hosea regarding Gomer? (Sing a few, if you
wish!)

Loyal Love

God told the prophet Hosea to go marry a
faithless woman. He did! Hosea chose
Gomer, who was described as a "wife of
whoredom"—possibly a prostitute or harlot
(Hosea 1:2-3). This union was a symbolic
act; Hosea was acting on God's behalf to
portray the faithful husband (God) pursuing
a faithless wife (Israel) and entreating her to
turn away from wicked ways. Her "children
of whoredom" symbolized the running after
other gods by the children of Israel.

So Hosea endured the shame of Gomer's
infidelity and
the disgrace of
illegitimate
offspring.
Hosea's anger
boiled. He threa-
tened to humil-
iate his wife
publicly while,
at the same
time, trying to
reel her in
(2:1-13).
Then Hosea
wooed Gomer
again and took
her to himself
as his wife for-
ever (2:14-23).
He faithfully
sealed their
love and claimed
the children as
his own. Hosea
willingly kept
love as a goal,
and it directed
all his actions.

Sacrificial Love

Hosea's case study marriage continues to juxtapose indiscriminate and faithful love. The text continues to track the actions of Hosea and his intent to renew and restore his relationship with Gomer.

Hosea 3:2 claims that Hosea bought Gomer with silver, grain, and wine. Maybe this was the cost of rescuing her from prostitution; she evidently belonged to someone else. Perhaps it was some civil hoop to be jumped through for Hosea to reclaim his bride. The price paid to get her back might be just another one of those acts of "family diplomacy." Nevertheless, Hosea bought Gomer with love and for a price. His sacrifice forgave and saved Gomer. It redeemed and reconciled their marital relationship.

God's *hesed* is sacrificial. In addition to this prophet's claim, consider a Gospel witness (John 3:16) and the conclusions of an early church elder (1 Peter 1:18-21). No judgment or condemnation, just a door of hope for all who claim the promises of love.

Nurturing Love

Hosea shifts his metaphoric human case study relationship from adulterous wife and loving husband to rebellious child and caring parent (Hosea 11).

The emphasis in this three-part—past, present, future—metaphor is God's nurturing love. In the past, Parent God had taught the young one to walk, carried and healed the child, and bent down to care. The child grew rebellious. He became more inclined to turn the other way than to answer when the Parent called.

The threat of "returning to Egypt"—its physical up-rooting, demands of back-breaking slave labor, and the loss of dignity

BIBLE

Sacrificial Love
Read Hosea 3. Bought with love and for a price—Hosea offers a sacrifice. How extreme is a love that offers a sacrifice on behalf of one who we think does not deserve to be loved? What implicit promises are tied to such a sacrifice?

God gave up the Son, which can be understood as a blood sacrifice. How extreme is this love? What promises are made firm by this sacrifice? What would you sacrifice for the love of God? for the love of your life? for the love of your spouse?

SMALL GROUP

Nurturing Love
Read Hosea 11:1-11. Reflect on this profound parental love. How does a patient and corrective love develop and cultivate reconciliation? What promises are made to make such nurturing love a reality?

and freedom—seemed to have no impact on Israel, characterized here as a disobedient child. Deuteronomic law suggests that such a rebellious child deserved to be condemned and stoned.

Now the child is being disciplined and the parent-child relationship is severely strained. But an intense parental love gets triggered by the suffering of the son. Overwhelming compassion, and the nurturing bond between the parent and defiant child, saves the child from destruction and death. The Parent, unable to destroy out of anger, nurtures and redirects the child back home.

Nurturing Love: A Journal Entry

Suzu probably shouldn't have wasted any more time on me! I had brought dishonor to her and to members of her household. She summoned me to her home. I arrived prepared to express my humble regret. She met me at the door. We sat face-to-face at a table set for tea. She spoke with wisdom about misdeeds in her own life and labored to understand what I could barely explain about my life. She offered admonition and counsel that I cherish to this day.

Healing Love

It is as if God is engaged in a landfill reclamation project. The piles of foul-smelling human sinfulness, transgression trash, and defiant debris have all been bulldozed under by God's sure love. The garbage that once threatened life has been replaced by a rich new seed medium. Here on this land, God's healing love renews, recovers, and reintroduces life.

The adulterous wife, the rebellious son, the wayward Israel return to God. Their disloyalty is healed. They have all returned to the land and been restored. God provides life-giving protection and nourishment and the people thrive and flourish.

CHOSEN LOVE

God called the people of Israel holy and, of all the peoples on earth, God chose them to be a treasured possession. God's heart was set on them (Deuteronomy 7:6-8). God's love is a chosen love. This love was intentionally cultivated for commitment. God chose Israel again and again and willingly acted out of love—far beyond the promises and duty of the covenant.

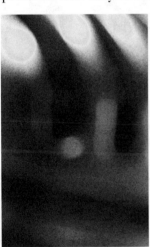

We pit the competing lovers of success, status, and self-importance against this loyal love of God. We resist the fishhook of love that God casts into our hearts. But God aches to claim us and welcome us home. God never lets go.

INSEPARABLE LOVE

In his letter to the Romans, Paul demonstrates and claims God's abundant and inseparable love. His reasoning makes it easy to welcome this love. God offered the Son, Jesus, as a sacrifice—is there anything

Chosen Love
Think about your own story. Characterize your own experience of God's sure love. See how your experience connects with the experience of the psalmist and metaphors in Hosea. Interpret and claim God's loyal, sacrificing, nurturing, and healing love in your own life.

No one is obligated to share personal stories until he or she is ready. For all responses, seek to understand, ask questions to clarify, honor differences, keep confidences, expect authenticity, offer accountability, foster trust, and resist the temptation to counsel.

Use these questions to help integrate your own experience with the Scripture: What competing lovers do you chase after? What tactics can you claim as part of God's plan to get you back? How does your experience of pain, disappointment, confusion, frustration, or even despair fit with the nurturing action of Parent God? What promises have been made firm by the loving actions of God in your life? Now, what do you believe about God's love?

Inseparable Love
Read Romans 8:31-39. Paul makes a list of powers (Romans 8:35) that can never separate us from the love of God in Christ Jesus. Make your own reality-based list of contemporary, day-to-day "powers" that can dominate your life. Take a moment to jot down the list of "powers." Then check the list against the wide bounds of God's steadfast love that Paul provides.

God wouldn't give? No! God and the Christ, the very ones who could accuse and condemn, don't! Instead, they protect the chosen ones in love (Romans 8:31-39).

In fact, no reality can force our separation from God. No reality can frustrate God's care and love for us. Things go badly sometimes. We can be victims of our own reality, impulses, bad choices, and ignorance. The "powers that be" that can dominate us. We may even be tempted to point to the bad times as proof that God has rejected, deserted, or abandoned us. But God's love cannot be hung up by the sway of these powers. God's power is almighty and God's love is boundless. Nothing that happens during our life can have a negative effect on God's sure love!

GOING FORTH

A Litany of Affirmation

God's love is a sure love. It is a faithful and nurturing love that forgives and heals. God's love is chosen, promised, cultivated, and sealed by the sacrificial blood of Christ.

Close with a litany of affirmation that claims this precious love. Use Paul's statement of faith at the end of Romans 8:39 as the refrain of the litany: "[Nothing] . . . will be able to separate us from the love of God in Christ Jesus our Lord."

Going Forth
Fashion this litany of affirmation by alternating between your list of "powers that be" and the statement of faith from Romans 8. Begin with Paul's statement. Then offer one "power" from your list of "powers that be" and respond together with the words of the refrain. Continue to alternate Paul's statement with "powers that be" until the list of powers has been depleted.

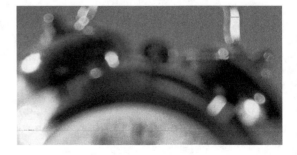

A SELF THAT LOVES

> This session is designed to claim the need to develop a self that can freely offer and accept love.

GETTING STARTED

Nicole: I get so engrossed in what other people think they want or need from me that I forget myself. Like when I meet someone new, I do everything with that other person in mind. I lose track of me.

Dannikka: I haven't exactly lived my life according to the "Good Book," and I'm not very proud of me. Even though I've put most of that behind me, some days I'm haunted by some of that ugliness; I can't even stand to look at myself in the mirror.

Amie: I've been hurt so many times. Sometimes I've been injured by what was done, and other times I've been wounded by what was not done. It's really difficult for me to trust anyone. I'm not convinced that love is really worth the effort.

Lee: I want to care for others and be there for them. I like to be needed and really hate to let people down. But if I don't care for me first, then everybody ends up mad.

Justis: I have this image that I just have to live up to. I expect a lot of me. I'm not sure where it comes from, but it controls everything I do

START Greet each other. Welcome and identify any newcomers. Invite each other to offer a brief "life since we last met" update.

CASE STUDY

Getting Started

Meet Nicole, Dannikka, Amie, Lee, and Justis. React to their perceptions and observations. Consider each self-identity as they are portrayed. How is it with their spirit and soul? Speculate on their ability to offer and receive love.

Perhaps you are familiar with the likeness of one or more of these persons. Use your imagination to develop their stories. Start with one or two sentences beyond these brief self-portraits. Feel free to add details throughout this and other sessions in this text.

Read Leviticus 19:2 and 1 Peter 1:13-25. How does the Bible describe holiness and what does it require of the believer? How does one become holy?

Holiness is both a model and a motivating force. To be holy is to imitate God.
- If Dannikka were to recognize her own holiness, how might she see herself when she looks in the mirror?
- How might holiness inform Nicole's relationships with others?
- If Justis were to embrace the wisdom of holiness, what might happen to that image he has to live up to?

Holiness
Much of Leviticus contains what we call the "Holiness Code," directions for holy living. Read through portions of Leviticus, particularly Chapters 19–21 to see the laws that set Israel apart and made the nation "pure" and holy.

Kind and Merciful
Read Luke 6:32-36. In this passage the question is not "Who should I love?" but "How should I love?"

and how I do it. When I can't keep up the image, I turn on myself. Sometimes, I even do things that undermine my own best efforts.

IN THE IMAGE AND LIKENESS

Since the beginning, humankind has been created in the image of God and blessed by the Creator. Genesis 1 proclaims that there is a relationship between God and all of God's creation. But, the relationship between God and humankind is different. God actually speaks to the human creatures (". . . and God said to them" [Genesis 1:28])! This is an intimate relationship.

Humanness carried within it the image of God. Human beings attest to the nature of God. Of course, we recognize that we see in the mirror only dimly. But how is it that humans are like God?

Holiness

As ones created in the likeness of God, holiness is a part of our human nature. That means that we are able to recognize the sacred, perceive that which can be claimed as hallowed, and honor those whom we know to be blessed. We have the capacity to respond to everything that strikes us as mysterious or awesome . . . to all that is holy.

Kind and Merciful

God's love is radical! It is unearned and totally undeserved. As children of the Most High, the character of our Parent God is to be reflected in us. To be kind is to couple gentleness and compassion with habits of generosity. Mercy is personified by patient forgiveness and is practiced with affectionate devotion. We are called to extend limitless kindness and mercy. Jesus claims that we are to love with kindness and mercy. As children of God, we can mirror this love in our relationship with our own self, as well as with others.

Chosen and Beloved

Not only are we created in the image of God and reflect God's likeness in love, we are chosen and beloved, too! We are intentionally chosen by God to be the recipients of God's sure love. At our baptism, we are called sons and daughters of God. This is our identity. We are who God says we are.

A Prayer From Dannikka's Journal

God, you know all that I know and call me holy. You love me when I can't even look myself in the eye in the mirror and appreciate any part of me. You know me and offer unlimited mercy. I know me and all I can do is despise me.

Look and see the emptiness, the hopelessness, and the anger. Then let me see me as you see me. Show me what it means to be patient with myself. Show me the forgiveness you once revealed to a woman caught in adultery. Teach me to offer that liberating power of forgiveness and pardon to me.

It seems so strange that you could love me so. Knock this disbelief and my inability to love me right out from underneath me. Let me be in your love. Let me embrace myself with that same unconditional, never-ending love. In utter gratitude and with heart-felt praise, I pray. Amen.

What does this Scripture urge you to do or to be? Do you think it's possible to follow these commands? Which seems the easiest for you? the hardest? Explain your answers.

- What if Lee could claim that loving self with kindness is not selfish but is really needed to care for others? How might that support what Lee already knows about himself?
- It seems obvious that it would be a challenge for Amie to be merciful with those who have hurt her. But what if Amie loved herself with mercy?

Chosen and Beloved Read Colossians 3:12-17. As God's chosen and beloved, pray your own way through the instructions first offered to Christians in Colossae. Pick up your journal or sit with a trusted friend for prayer.

As you read this Scripture, acknowledge whether you are able to see yourself as holy. Own any inadequate efforts to mirror God's compassion, gentle kindness, and love with your own spirit and celebrate the light that you do have. Pray that you might be patient with yourself. Ask to reflect God's forgiving spirit in your own life. Give thanks for your identity as a son or daughter, created in the image and likeness of God.

Close this time of prayer with a praise chorus or other song of faith.

A Self That Loves

YOU BELONG TO ME

We live in a "you belong to me" world. The "me" corresponds to all our relationships with friends and family, work demands, school load, and all the other products of our competitive and status-seeking society.

Instead of describing the value and worth of our own self according to the likeness and kinship of God, we may find ourselves being defined by the "me" powers: possessions, the status or quality of our work, judgments of what is "good" (prosperity and greed) and "bad" (guilt and failure), and especially our relationships with others. All of these "me" powers threaten us and try to force us to give up our God-given identity. How can we keep this reality from defining our spirit?

A Foolish Farmer

Jesus told a story of a foolish farmer who became identified with all the "gotta haves" in his life. The rich farmer succumbed to the lure of bigger barns, more stuff, and life in the lap of luxury. He considered himself to be a self-made man and took all the credit for his bin-busting harvest. He thought he had it made. But then, suddenly he died. Now, what good was all his stuff? It went to someone else.

What good does it do to gain the whole world but lose your own soul? The stuff of the "you belong to me" world takes life away.

A Foolish Farmer
Read Luke 12:13-21. Use a Bible commentary to understand all the intricacies of the story. The farmer belongs to a world built on possessions, self-sufficiency, pride, greed, and pleasure-seeking. He hoards and lives completely for himself.

Peel away the layers of this Gospel account one at a time. Consider the question of estate settlement, application of the law, and greed as the context for the parable. Then listen to the parable as a member of the crowd. What provoked God's judgment of "fool"? Specifically, what actions led to the judgment? Is any one of the rich man's actions more corrupt than the others, or was it simply the accumulation of misdeeds? What human character and feelings does the moral of the parable (verse 21) appeal to?

INTERNAL ENEMIES

Besides all the external relationships, demands, and obligations, there are also internal enemies that try to obscure our own God-given identity. Our own will can turn against us, attack us, and effectively compel us to "give up" our spirit.

Our self and its identity can be held hostage by envy or resentment. Anger can impair our ability to act or decide. Rage and irritability link us to power struggles, distrust, and manipulative relationships. Depression and hopelessness have the capacity to skew our habits, feelings, and attitudes. Obsessions, compulsive behaviors, and addictions may motivate violent actions of self-hatred or self-contempt.

Remember Justis

Justis is in his mid-twenties. He is an energetic and highly principled person with a great deal of ambition and ingenuity. Justis has always been driven—not by any kind of standard for success or by personal accomplishments as much as this "something" inside him that pushes perfection.

Justis has an integral part in his family's business, but is in no way guaranteed a job. He's at school in the morning three days a week and works the balance of those days and

SMALL GROUP

Internal Enemies
These internal enemies can blind us to who we are. A worst-case scenario finds us taking on the role of God and passing judgment against our own self. Then fear, guilt, and failure further shadow our ability to love.

Sit with a couple of others you trust and listen to one another. Identify and describe your own distorted habits of seeing, feeling, thinking, and acting that blind you to who you are as a child of God. How do these habits diminish your ability to love?

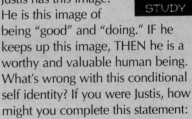

Remember Justis
Justis has this image. He is this image of being "good" and "doing." IF he keeps up this image, THEN he is a worthy and valuable human being. What's wrong with this conditional self identity? If you were Justis, how might you complete this statement: "IF only I _____ more, THEN I would be a "better" person."

What are the consequences of Justis's push for perfection? What habits of seeing, feeling, thinking, and acting would you notice if you spent time with Justis?

How do these habits meddle with God's call to be holy and to love with kindness and mercy? Attempt to answer Justis's questions from your own experience.

B
I
B
L
e

One Self
Read from this Luke sampler:

- Jesus' baptism (3:21-22)
- Jesus' temptation (4:1-13)
- Jesus' authority to forgive sins (5:17-26)
- Jesus at table with outcasts (5:29-32)
- Jesus and the sabbath laws (6:6-11)
- The woman who was a sinner (7:36-50)

You may choose to spend time with one or more of the Scripture passages independently, in pairs, or in break-out groups. Use these questions as discussion starters:

- Who is this Jesus? How do the actions of Jesus embrace and identify the love that is the heart and character of God? How do these actions defy the "me" powers?
- The religious leaders and Jesus are devoutly committed to competing obligations: upholding social and religious traditions versus meeting the needs of humanity. How do they reconcile these differences? Explain how this struggle might inspire a spirit to grow in the likeness of God's love.
- What happens to the characters caught in the crossfire between Jesus and the religious authorities? The actions of these characters prompt both "good" and "bad" judgments. How do such mixed judgments nurture a self to grow in love?

all the rest. He is a trained EMT/paramedic and volunteers with the local fire department.

He talks about being saved and called by a God who is always there. But he obviously doesn't get it. Sometimes he fears himself. He's afraid in the face of his own anger, fearful when he directs that anger at himself, petrified when the anger gets flung at those he loves.

One day Justis wondered aloud:

"Why do I do things that hurt me? Sometimes something goes clunk in my head and I turn on myself. How can I love me? How can I know any love when my head sends me hate mail with every breath?"

ONE SELF DEVELOPED TO LOVE

At his baptism, Jesus is announced as who God says he is: God's beloved Son (Luke 3:21). This Son of God did not come with military might to overthrown the prevailing powers. Jesus came to fulfill the Law and the Prophets. He healed on the sabbath, ate with sinners, spoke to women, and claimed authority to forgive sins.

Jesus freely offered and accepted love. Central to the objections and accusations of the Pharisees, lawyers, and synagogue leaders was Jesus' self-giving love. Jesus did not let his self identity be defined by the expectations of the Pharisees and other "me" powers of his day. He did not let the condemnation of the elders, chief priests, and scribes force him to give up his God-given spirit. He did not yield to deceptive images of self or give in and turn judgment on himself. He successfully foiled the temptations by the greatest "me" power, Satan, the tempter or the evil one (Luke 4:1-13).

ONE SELF SAVED TO LOVE

Love of God and others cannot grow from self-hatred. There cannot be love where there is no self to do the loving. Yet, our ability to love is a part of our created nature—it can never be completely lost. No matter how damaged our identity, how obscure our reality, or how twisted our habits of seeing, feeling, thinking, and acting—we can trust that God is always moving to save the holy that is in us. God loves us so we can love, and God urges us toward love.

One Self Saved to Love: A Journal Entry

God, you've made me a survivor! You found my heart, touched it, and called me your own. Your boundless love moved me from despair to hope, from harming to healing, from death to life. You rescued me from me!

You offer life, a way of being that is love. You shower me with love; a gentle love full of mercy and forgiveness, a love of grace that knows no end. I am so grateful. How can I "make good" on your love? I've been saved from me. My life is yours.

SEEK TO LOVE

We are called to love. We are called as chosen ones, created in the image and likeness of a loving God. But we have to make a conscious decision to claim our identity and seek to offer and accept love.

If we seek to love, we commit a whole lifetime to closing the gap between the decision to *be* a loving self and *becoming* a lov-

A Journal Entry
Pick up your journal or sit with one or two trusted friends. How do you "hate away" or "give away" or "If—then away" your God-given self and spirit? When has God boldly loved and worked to save the holy in you? What action does this love require of you?

Seek to Love
What "me" powers and inner enemies must you choose to give up?

What relationships need to end (or change) so that you can claim an identity that can freely offer and accept love?

Read Luke 9:23-27. (The "cross to take up" is not an inconvenience to overcome but a sacrifice to be made.) What will you "take up" on the way to *becoming* a loving self?

A Self That Loves

ing self. We will not always live up to this holy image and may even be tempted to bully ourselves when we fail. It is not a once-and-for-all heroic transformation willed by a finger snap and realized in the blink of an eye. It is pursued. The development of an identity that loves requires action and effort.

Seeking to love means opposing the self that is defined by "me" powers and inner

enemies. It involves laying down a life that may really belong to someone else and taking up a new identity in the likeness of God and the Son, Jesus. It assumes that action will be in sync with a decision to love. In Luke 9:23-27, Jesus challenged all who want to be followers to deny themselves, take up their cross, and follow. Those who seek to love are followers!

GOING FORTH

Me? Identified with the image and likeness of God? Me? A holy self, chosen and beloved? Yes! At our baptism God tells us who we are. Each time we meet at God's table we are told who we are.

We can't earn the identity of one who loves. Our capacity to freely offer and accept love is made real by God's sure love. All we have to do is trust God's word about who we are and get reacquainted with that person. All we have to do is develop our own self and grow our own spirit in love.

THOSE WE CALL FRIENDS

> This session will explore the actions, characteristics, and love of friends.

GETTING STARTED

When you're reading a newspaper, how long does it take you to flip to the funnies? In just a few frames cartoonists can unlock the mysteries of human relationships, comment on reality, and hold up a mirror so we can see.

THE FUNNIES SPEAK

Friendship is a common relationship among comic strip characters. Some of the friends have been together for the long haul, such as Lucy, Linus, Charlie Brown, Sally, and other members of the "Peanuts" gang; the stereotypical girl Margaret and the all-boy "Dennis the Menace"; and everybody's next door neighbors—Blondie, Dagwood, Tootsie, and Herb. There are some new friends in the funnies, too! Kid friends Agnes and her best friend Trout, teen friends Jeremy and Hector (in "Zits"), live-in friends in "Apartment 3-G," and mom friends Wanda and Bunny in "Baby Blue's."

START

Greet each other. Welcome and identify any newcomers. Invite each other to offer a brief "life since we last met" update.

DISCUSS

The Funnies
Choose a favorite from your comic strip friends. Cut out a recent daily strip and cover up the words in the speech balloons, or just picture the friends being together in four frames. Create your own crisp dialogue and punch lines for these comic strip friends. Use the characters to capture a truth or point out the obvious about friendship. Tap your own experiences, insights, blessings, hurts, and deepest desires.

Friendship Wisdom
Read Proverbs 17:17;
18:24; 27:10 . If you
have a Bible with an
Apocrypha, read Sirach 6:5-17;
9:10; 22:19-26; 37:1-6.

What does the Wisdom literature
say about friendship? What conditions foster true friendship? What
circumstances cause friends to
slip away? What are characteristics of a false friendship and how
do you recognize them?

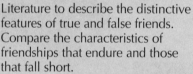

Wisdom Literature
Use your own comic
strip wisdom and that
of the Wisdom
Literature to describe the distinctive
features of true and false friends.
Compare the characteristics of
friendships that endure and those
that fall short.

FRIENDSHIP WISDOM

Friends are freely chosen on the basis of
their personal qualities. They want the
same things and hold the same values that
we do. They see and come
about the same truths. They
make and keep promises.

Friends walk side-by-
side with us. Good friends
are good for us. They speak
and listen fully, openly, and
without fear. True friends
have the capacity to care for
our well-being, help us realize our deepest desires, and
even heal us.

False friends can be more
a detriment than a benefit.
They might over-step relational boundaries
or use others to meet their own selfish
needs. They may be unfaithful or uneven in
their commitment.

Biblical Studies 101
Wisdom Literature
Wisdom Literature instructs, solves problems, and hands down specific traditions.
The books of Proverbs and Sirach offer practical lessons for coping with life based
on real-life experience. The writers lift up standards and motivation for conduct,
such as honesty, self-control, and diligence. The actions of the wise and the foolish
are often pitted against each other to furnish the context for advice and counsel.
Sirach ("Ecclesiasticus" or the "Wisdom of Ben Sira") is classified as an Apocryphal
text by Protestants. The writer is a private school teacher. Most of Sirach consists of
short, instructional passages regarding good living. These lines and paragraphs
embrace a variety of subjects related to the human experience. The truths in the text
readily elicit the agreement of its readers. The language patterns and cadences of the
verses make the wisdom memorable.

MY FRIENDS,
MY ENEMIES

Job experienced a great deal of human
suffering. His friends came to him out of

compassion and sought to console and comfort him. Eliphaz, Bildad, and Zophar expressed their solidarity with Job just by being present with him in his suffering. Their gestures and tears communicated their own grief and distress. Without uttering a word they sympathized and were in sorrow with him (Job 1–2). By all appearances Eliphaz, Bildad, and Zophar were to be counted as three of Job's true friends.

Throughout most of the rest of the Book of Job, the three friends began to talk. Each friend spoke to Job, in order, one at a time. Job, in turn, mustered a rebuttal to each speech. Eliphaz confronted Job and maintained that he had lost sight of who he really was—that Job's anger toward God was "not like him." Bildad called Job to repent for his sins and to do something to win back God. Zophar accused Job of both sin and empty-headed stupidity. The speeches continued until finally Job was accused of wickedness.

The verbal "tit for tat" dialogue between Job and his friends turned nasty, curt, and sarcastic. Job condemned the three for their failure as friends. He told Eliphaz, Bildad, and Zophar that they were good-for-nothing comforters and testified that they made him feel worse—not better! Job accused them of verbal beatings, false accusations, and slander. He scolded them for their faulty convictions and hollow words.

God gets the last word with the friends (and with Job). God spoke with angry criticism and called for a burnt offering. Job interceded with God on behalf of Eliphaz, Bildad, and Zophar and they were reconciled with God.

AMIE

I grew up in an abusive household. I didn't do anything to deserve it—it's just the hand

SMALL GROUP

Friends, Enemies
Skim Job 1:1–2:10 to set the scene for the drama between Job and his friends. Read Job 2:11-13 together. Then form two break-out groups. Group One will read Job 4:1-6; 8:1-7; 11:2-12 on the tone of the three friends. Group Two will read Job 16:1-5; 19:1-3; 21:34 on life as Job sees it.

Stage your own daytime talk show called "Can This Friendship Be Saved?" Select a host to preside and mediate and a panel of the three friends and Job. Alternate these interview suggestions for the host between Job and his friends:
- To the three friends: What did you assume about the plight and needs of Job? How did you expect to meet those needs?
- To Job: What did you need from your friends? How well did they meet your needs?

The next few questions will test the panel's willingness and interest for reconciliation:
- To Job: What do you wish your friends would say or do now? How willing are you to accept their action and counsel?
- To the three friends: How willing are you to meet Job's needs? What will you say and do now?

Improvise the show's ending and then process the outcome. Ask the observers: How realistic is the hope of reconciliation for this friendship? What factors cancel out any hope of ever being friends again? What factors sustain the possibility of reestablishing these bonds?

Amie
When friends understand what they do, they can reflect the image of God's reliable and loving presence. Imagine yourself in Amie's situation. What would you say to your friends? What would you want your friends to say or do on your behalf? How might you talk to Amie about how her friendship with Jamal could turn to love and what the difference would be?

To Be Betrayed
Pick up your journal or sit with a trusted friend. Talk about your own experiences of being betrayed. Be specific about your feelings no matter how intense.

Use Psalm 55:12-23 as a means to vent your feelings to God in prayer. Include an affirmation of your trust in God's love and power, then close with a praise chorus or other song of faith.

I've been dealt. I'm not the only victim, but I still don't make a big deal about it. When I was younger I tried telling other family members, teachers, and a few of my closest friends what was really happening with me. But often, what they did and what they said injured me more than I was being hurt at home. The whole experience has added up to some real mistrust for me.

Right now I'm sharing an apartment with some people I would call friends. They really care for me. In fact, I think I would marry Jamal tomorrow if our friendship ever went that way. What if I were to open up and confide in them? How do I say that I need to learn how to trust so that they will understand? How can I ask those closest to me to speak and act in ways that might really help?

BLATANT BETRAYAL

Our lives are so connected with friends. We rely on them for support and trust them with some of our deepest needs. In the instant one friend betrays us, we may wonder if all of our other friends become unreliable, too! Without tried and true friends, our lives can be threatened.

To Be Betrayed

The psalmist has been betrayed by one of his closest friends. The prevailing conditions in this life are obviously chaotic, but the specific act(s) of disloyalty are uncertain. The unreliability of humans only serves to strengthen the psalmist's trust in God.

To Betray

The Gospels narrate the charade of Judas the conspirator (Matthew 26:14-16, 47-56). Jesus was not taken by surprise, despite whatever secrecy surrounded Judas's action. Judas met Jesus at night, and Jesus played right into his plan. An enemy used a gesture of a friend's affection as a weapon. A friend drew his sword like an enemy. Then everyone abandoned Jesus.

LOYAL FRIENDS

David and Jonathan shared a deep and abiding friendship. It was a personal pact. This intimate friendship was grounded in covenant with God. The decisions and actions that backed their commitments were made with great risk and undertaken at a price. This friendship strained beyond the present to embrace a larger vision—a "wide angle" loyalty that bound them to each other, to their future descendants, and to Israel.

At first, David was the one in danger and he sought Jonathan's help. Then, the tables turned and Jonathan needed the assurance of David's *hesed*—for himself and his immediate household. The promises were played out with a practical, obligatory human *hesed*—an unwavering love and loyalty that would be both offered and received.

HUMAN HESED

The same "steadfast love," "faithfulness," and "loyalty" that characterizes God's *hesed* is also known in the context of relationships among humans—kin, hosts and guests, friends and allies, rulers and their subjects. It's an action-based, duty-bound, obligatory, and practical pattern of human behavior. *Hesed* is practiced by situationally superior parties who act on behalf of the helpless. The one who acts rec-

To Betray
Read Matthew 26:14-16, 47-56. Add to the story based on your own experiences as betrayers. Recount the behind-the-scenes scheming and collusion, the moment of betrayal, the after-effects. Was the violence really intended? Was the eventual denial by Peter and the desertion of the others part of Judas's master plan? Was Judas delighted or mortified by the total unraveling of Jesus' disciples and friends? Was Jesus' abandonment more proof of a mission accomplished or a conspiracy reeling out-of-control?

Loyal Friends
Read 1 Samuel 20:12-17 and 2 Samuel 9:1-7.
These two linked stories explain by example the pain of loyalty, the essential qualities of human *hesed,* and the levitical commandment to love neighbor as self .
Practically speaking, what behavior did Jonathan expect from David? Why did he ask? Why couldn't Jonathan expect security from his own house?

Even as his power was destroying the house of Saul, David still sought to make good on his promises and perform *hesed.* What happened when David and Mephibosheth met with their collective hurts, hates, fears, and hopes?

Human *Hesed*

What commitment in the life of this pastor might have motivated her to carry out *hesed* with Dannikka? How important is her action in Dannikka's life? How has Dannikka responded to this pastor's faithfulness?

Describe a time when someone has acted on your behalf. It might have been a friend, a classmate, a co-worker or colleague, or someone who knows another member of your family clan. How did you respond to this expression of loyalty and affection? Who might be crying out to you to act with *hesed*?

Biblical Studies 101: Human Hesed

Stories of Old Testament persons and their relationships such as, Abraham and Sarah (Genesis 12:10-13; 20:9-13), Joseph and his brothers (Genesis 47:29-31), Rahab and the spies (Joshua 2:1-14), and Hushai and Absalom (2 Samuel 16:15-19) illustrate this faithful love—this human *hesed*.

ognizes some responsibility to respond to the one in need. The one performing *hesed*, though free to decide not to act, usually fulfills an important need. The action is often something that the one in need could not possibly have done alone and may even be something that only that actor could do. *Hesed* keeps and protects the fidelity of human relationships.

Human *Hesed*: An Entry From Dannikka's Journal

After months of failed attempts to walk into the church to get the help I so desperately needed, I finally made it in as far as the pastor's office. She wasn't there. I left a note asking for time. She called and agreed to meet me for lunch without asking me why.

I told her the tale of my tangled web and my own self-hatred. She offered immediate grace. She heard it all, claimed the "seriousness" of what she'd heard, and agreed to see me and seek care for me. Later, I tried to give her a way out, but she didn't back away! She's posed tough questions, offered hope, walked with me through my darkness, and pointed to God's love there, even in the dark!

She didn't have to call me. She didn't even have to agree to meet me. But, she did, and she heard my cries as one who has been there. She continues to act on my behalf and for my sake.

GROWING IN LOVE

You are a child of God. You know yourself to be in God's love. This love includes those whom God has created and whom you call friends.

It takes a lifetime to grow in love. Our friends are our guinea pigs and we are their lab rats. We can gesture with kindness and criticize with our tongue. We can affirm differences in one setting and betray our friends in our next breath. We can show comfort to our friends, but then we want it to be "our turn." We can forgive our friends as long as they still owe us. We can be trusted until we need the information about our friends to meet our own needs. We can claim to be faithful and then run the other way when our friends are in trouble.

Listen as Lee, Kurt, Paki, James, and Lisha talk about the relationship they have with their friends.

Lee: I would do anything for my really good friends. It seems like the more stress and pressure we have in our lives, the closer and stronger we get.

Kurt: I've got good friends, and suddenly they've scattered all over the globe! You don't realize how much you love them until you aren't around them . . . as in 2,200 miles away. E-mail, phone calls, and cyberspace chat is OK some of the time. But sometimes I really could use somebody right here "on-the-spot" with me.

Paki: My intimate relationship was taking control of my whole life. One night, when I told her that I was going out, I realized that I had no friends. So I decided to make some friends, and then she got angry that I wanted to spend time with them and not with her.

James: I have a friend for every occasion

Growing in Love
Answer the following questions based on the brief descriptions that Lee, Kurt, Paki, James, and Lisha offered. What distinctive characteristics of true friendship does each one seem to hold? What are some of the enemies of friendship that are revealed? What qualities of true friendship might each one seek to grow?

How would you describe the relationship you share with your friends? Reflect personally on the three questions asked of Lee, Kurt, Paki, James, and Lisha. Claim at least one quality of true friendship that you need to grow into.

Begin to help one another to be accountable to the group for your own growth in love. As your group continues to meet, be prepared to honestly report the success and challenges of your life as it grows in the qualities of human love. Create a trusting, supportive, and nurturing environment. Invite one another to listen carefully, not scold, criticize, put-down, or judge one another's "success." Consider asking other group members for prayers, specific support, gentle challenges, ideas/approaches, and resources to tap to meet your growth goal(s).

and social function. I have friends that drink and others that dance. I have some that clean up real nice and make me look real good. I think they'd all say I'm their friend, but I sure hope they don't expect anything from me!

Lisha: I am looking for that one-in-a-thousand treasure—someone I could honor as a friend for life. I would cherish a kindred soul relationship that could truly engage two hearts. I would value an intimate bond with someone else, so we could be like sisters.

LOOK CLOSER

Covenant Discipleship

Covenant Discipleship groups meet to wait and watch over each other in love and become better disciples of Jesus Christ. Group members are trustworthy and supportive, not judgmental. Leadership is shared and relationships are nurtured and developed as members learn to listen and respect one another. In its purest form, the life of these groups are bound by a covenant that embraces compassion, devotion, justice, and worship. Contact: Steve Manskar; 1-877-899-2780, extension 1765 (toll free); e-mail *smanskar@gbod.org.* for more information.

CLOSE

Going Forth

Sit down in the presence of friends and in the presence of God. In silence, meet God as you might meet your best friend. Share a few private moments together. Experience God's holy presence.

Close with spontaneous prayers that can be heard by others. Give thanks for God's holy presence. Invite that same presence into your human relationships. Ask for the Spirit's power to grow in love.

After prayers, exchange signs of Christian love.

GOING FORTH

The people Israel desired a God who was near to them and not "off somewhere." Their need for an ever-present and personal God was the tension behind the whole golden calf affair (Exodus 32). Then a chapter later (Exodus 33:7-11), they witnessed their God speaking face-to-face with Moses. The relationship between God and Moses was very close. They spoke openly and intimately as true friends (33:11).

AROUND THE FAMILY CIRCLE

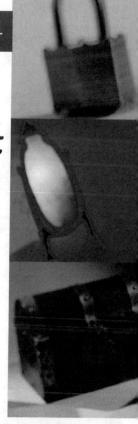

This session will look at family membership, household living, kin loyalty, and the transforming power of familial love.

SETTING STARTED

In your mind's eye, picture yourself at age ten. You are sitting down at a table and eating an evening meal with family. What shape is the table? Who is sitting where? Why? How is the meal thing happening? Who's running around setting the table, doing the cooking, putting food on the plates, and getting the milk? After it's all over, who will clean up?

Try to remember another evening from your ten-year-old days. On this night, company is coming! Who might be coming? Are they welcomed to the table as "family" or as "guests?" Is there any difference? If so, what?

START Greet each other. Welcome and identify any newcomers. Invite each other to offer a brief "love grown since last we met" update. Feel free to ask for specific support and prayers. Be ready to honor requests for prayer and nurturing.

WHO IS MY FAMILY?

Jesus was inside a house and surrounded by a crowd. Some in the crowd told him that his mother and siblings were outside and asking for him. Jesus replied with an inquiry about the identity of his family members. Then, Jesus began casting believers in the roles of brothers, sisters, and mothers. Those inside were called by our conventional familial titles, those outside were not.

DISCUSS Share the details of your ten-year-old table experiences. Who were some of the people you claimed as "family" when you were ten? Think of your own table now. What shape is it? Where do you sit? Who are the people whom you welcome to this table and call "family?"

Jesus does not define family by blood. Instead, Jesus characterizes family as more of a circle in which persons are held in love. A family is where promises to love can be kept and persons can be loved into being as a child of God.

FAMILY LIFE

The story of Joseph is a captivating tale about a young man and his family. The story tells of the extremes of living in a human household where there is believing and deceiving, belonging and distancing, desire and disgust, and joy and grief. The plot twists and turns and takes the long way to hope and love.

Joseph was the son of Jacob and his beloved wife Rachel. Joseph was his father's favored son. But to his older half-brothers, he was an unwelcome afterthought! The other brothers vied for the affection of their father. Jacob's obsessive love for Joseph fueled the others' hatred of Joseph. This hatred caused strife, which drove this whole saga.

The brothers' smoldering anger, hatred, and jealousy hatched a plan of doom and deception. Joseph was eliminated (or so it

Love: Opening Your Heart to God and Others

seemed). His robe, once presented in love, was seized in hate. It became the evidence of death and a token of deceit. Jacob lamented, mourned, and refused to be comforted.

Roxanne

My folks had been married for almost forty years. They moved here a couple of years ago. Now I know that this move was all a part of a conniving plan to make sure Mom had family nearby and someone to care for her in her old age. Dad's apparently had a woman on the side for years and finally decided to chase after her. He left my Mom about a year ago. He hasn't bothered to communicate with me or our children (his beloved grandchildren) since then. In the meantime, I've gotten to sit here and watch my mother's anger and grief.

For months we didn't know whether Dad was dead or alive. Recently, Dad's been checking in with my eldest sister's husband through e-mail. I'd heard from my sister that Dad and the woman were buying a condo together and she speculated about whether they were married.

We need not wonder anymore. We got word of his upcoming nuptials after a distant and long-time friend of my dad's forwarded his e-mail invitation to my brother-in-law who, in turn, forwarded it to my husband. Not one word to me directly from my own father! Not one word directly to any of his own flesh and blood!

FAMILY LOYALTY

The Book of Ruth focuses on a single family. Elimelech, Naomi, and their two sons journeyed from Judah during a famine

SMALL GROUP

Consider your own experiences with household conflict and kin tensions. Focus on two incidents: one from your childhood and one that involves your present kin or household.
- Describe the players and their connections to each other.
- Identify the source of the discord.
- Explain the actions and feelings of those involved at the height of the conflict.
- Reflect on gains and losses, promises and dreams.

CASE STUDY

Use Roxanne's case or one of your own choosing to investigate family tensions. How can kin be family if there is no communication? How do betrayal and deceit encumber this family's communication? Dad has disengaged, but what about the rest of the clan? How might this crisis change Roxanne's family? How might she get her mother and her siblings to hold tight to the family circle so that the promises of love can be kept?

BIBLE

Family Loyalty
Read Ruth 2. This story focuses on family loyalty. Ruth clings and keeps close. What does it mean to "keep close?" How does closeness help to verify who is family and who's not? Who among these characters are family? Is Ruth considered family? Explain how outsiders get to belong and be claimed as family.

in the land. They settled in Moab where their sons took Moabite wives, Orpah and Ruth. In the span of about ten years, Naomi's husband and both of her sons died. Naomi began the journey back to Judah with her daughters-in-law. Naomi wanted Orpah and Ruth to turn back to their mothers' homes and to remarry. Orpah was persuaded by Naomi's arguments and kissed Naomi goodbye. Ruth clung to Naomi.

Ruth gave voice to an impassioned speech and refused to abandon Naomi. She said she would go with Naomi and make her own commitments to God and to God's chosen people. Ruth was not in anyway expected to remain with her mother-in-law. She had no obligation. Ruth's love and loyalty is human *hesed*.

Naomi sought out Boaz, a landowner and a distant relation on her husband's side. Boaz instructed Ruth to glean only in his field and to keep close to his young women. Boaz offered his food as a gesture of her inclusion and acceptance. He assumed the role of protector, performed *hesed*, and invoked God's blessing as he acknowledged Ruth's devotion to Naomi.

Keisha

I packed up and moved back home right after my husband Shawn's suicide. There were lots of reasons why I thought I had to leave and why it seemed like the right thing to do. I'm settling into a job in our family's business—the very job that Dad has always promised would be there for me if I ever needed it. I'm guessing that sooner or later folks around here will begin to remember that the middle Thomas child is a girl.

I've started seeing somebody. He's just boomeranged back home after serving enlistment duty in the Army. He plans to start using his GI Bill college scholarship funds in the fall. Would you believe it? On our first date, we left town to try to keep the local tongues from wagging and ran right into one of Shawn's old friends.

It's been eight months since Shawn's death. I think that I really might be in love again. Dad says this is all happening way too fast. Folks about town say it's way too soon.

FAMILY TRANSFORMED

Joseph

The young and powerless Joseph has become a mighty and calculating governor. He was under no obligation to meet his brothers' need for food. The brothers, locked fast by their past, were not free to meet Joseph's demands. Their father Jacob seemed unable to risk any more on behalf of the promises.

But the dead one was alive and the dream is being realized! Joseph acted in accord with God's faithfulness. Joseph made a clean break with the past and restored the family circle. The extremes of grief, hurt, and deception would soon give way to genuine joy and healing.

There's much more to this story than just human action and reaction. God made promises to Abraham and Jacob, to Israel. Everything that happened to Jacob and his house involved a whole nation and a people chosen by God. Everything that happened to Joseph and his brothers was put to use by God to make a way for these promises. Even enemies of the dream and the dreamer himself had a role in keeping the promises of God.

BIBLE

Joseph
In four small groups each read a chapter of Genesis 42–45. Briefly compare notes to get a sense of the whole story.

God is in, with, under, and behind all human actions—even brokenness! Trace the actions that led the brothers from hatred to reconciliation. What human emotions and actions did Joseph derail? What happened when the abuse of power turned into a use of power in ways that concurred with God's steadfast love?

C A S E STUDY

Use your imagination to develop Amie's testimony to God's loving presence and promises. How does Amie's experience witness to the transforming power of a family's everyday love? Look back on love and life in your own family of origin. Take advantage of 20/20 hindsight. How would you define your family's "everyday love"? Point to some of the ways that God was in, with, under, and behind your family's human actions. As you grew up, how were you shaped and formed by your family's everyday love?

SMALL GROUP

A Father's Love

Use a Bible commentary to dig into all the many nuances of this powerful story. Read Luke 15:11-32 aloud. Listen as if you are sitting among a crowd of "younger sons" as Jesus tells this parable. An "older son" might claim that the father's loving forgiveness condones the younger one's actions. What would a "younger son" claim?

An "older son" might maintain that the father's loving mercy—the robe, the ring, the party—erases the sin. What would a "younger son" maintain?

An "older son" might believe that the father's loving grace snubs him and is just not fair. What would a "younger son" believe?

Amie

My father provided our family with a legacy of abuse. I can remember when I discovered that our family's ways of being together were not the same as my friends' families. It took much longer for me to realize that fear, secrecy, and pain were not the standard by which others measured the quality of their family life. I truly believe that all families are frail—our family was just a little more brittle than some others.

I am grateful for my family. We have all lived into our family's legacy and have contributed to it in one way or another over the years. Sometimes we dreamed and sometimes we denied, but we always loved. Somehow God managed to keep the promises of love in all the agonizing humanness of my family.

A Father's Love

A father had two sons. The younger asked for his share of the inheritance. His request supposed death. He turned away from home and traveled to a distant country. His actions made him lost. The son severed bonds with his father.

The son really became lost. He was defeated, depraved, and destitute. He had a "heart-to-heart" talk with "the face in the mirror." He reckoned with himself. He saw his folly. He turned back toward home.

Once home, the son found that he could

not cut the cords of his father's love! His father's loving forgiveness demanded no confession or retribution. His father's loving mercy restored this son's identity. His father's loving grace reestablished his son's bonds of love.

GROWING IN LOVE

You are a child of God. You know yourself to be in God's love. This love includes those whom God has created and those whom you call friends and family.

It takes a lifetime to grow in love. We ask, "Are you family?" and then distance ourselves from those we invite into our circle. We make promises to hold the circle in love and then do everything in our power to cause strife. We try to love each other into becoming a child of God with anger, jealousy, and grief.

Amie's Talk With Jesus

Jesus, I heard you tell the story of a father's love—the loving forgiveness, mercy, and grace that changed everything!

Amie, do you know love?

Yeah, I do in spite of my father.

Love is the calm in the midst of a great storm. It's the grace of a good catch. It's being present with a woman you're not supposed to be seen with. It's the generosity of a little boy in a crowd. It's family around a table. Love transcends anger in the Temple; despair and desperate pleading in a garden; disappointment about promises broken, loyalties dashed, the kiss of a betrayer. It's peace at a moment of temptation. Endurance under duress. It's mercy for a criminal and forgiveness for all humanity.

SMALL GROUP

Amie's Talk
Pick up your journal or sit with a couple of trusted friends or kin. Like Amie, imagine that you have just heard Jesus tell the parable of the loving father. Call out Jesus' name and ask him to walk with you. Hear Jesus' voice and feel welcomed by his presence. Explore what it means to think you have to "measure up" with God. Dare to ask how God is in, with, under, and behind your own family's human actions. Confess your inability to hold the circle in love. Commit to grow a quality of human love in the context of family.

Write or speak about your talk with Jesus.

I know that love. It might even be because of my father. But . . . .

You can't trust the promises of love?

I want to know love. I want to find my own story in the book of love. I want to live in love. But how do I trust?

Ask. Ask God. Ask Love to plant trust in you, a trust that can make peace with your fears. Offer to nurture the trust planted, to cultivate it, and to tend it. Agree to give your whole life—heart, mind, body, spirit, and soul—to Love.

What if I don't—

Measure up? Love is the promise-keeper. Open your heart. Let Love be inscribed there. Then, trust that you will be Love's child.

GOING FORTH

Amie's Prayer

Sit down with Jesus. Write a short prayer asking God to plant and nurture one quality of human love in you. Offer to tend and grow your love.

Reassemble as a group and pray the prayers aloud. Begin by praying Amie's prayer and then continue with prayers around the circle. Close with the reading of Psalm 33:22 and offer one another signs of Christian love and caring.

Dear God, Love, and Promise-keeper, plant trust in me. Seed me with a trust that will make peace with my fears, placate my anxiety, and temper my self-hatred. Plant a trust that's true. Sow a trust that with our tending will grow into a trust that you can call good.

You will see this trust grow into an open heart. You will recognize my efforts to nurture this trust as I give grace freely and offer quick forgiveness. I will seek to tend this trust with a gentle spirit. You, O Love, will be my refuge, my shelter, my strength for all of my life. Amen.

COMMUNITY MANNERS

This session will look at loving neighbor and offering hospitality in and beyond the faith community.

GETTING STARTED

Play the "Die Game." Role a die. Briefly respond to the statement that corresponds with the number on the die.

1. Characterize the membership and function of a community.
2. Explain your understanding of the word *neighbor*.
3. Describe the scene captured in a photograph published with the caption "Loving Neighbor."
4. Tell about a song, phrase, or verse that helps remind you to act in love.
5. Describe the actions of someone who has welcomed you as a stranger and extended uncommon hospitality.
6. Specify two or three things that a community of faith must do because no one else will do it.

WE LOVE, WE LOVE NOT

The idea that love could be a construct around which everything else lives and thrives is a prevailing theme in Paul's let-

START Greet each other. Welcome and identify any newcomers. Invite each other to offer a brief "love grown since last we met" update. Feel free to ask for specific support and prayers. Be ready to honor requests for prayer and nurturing.

DISCUSS Work through the "Die Game" questions. Try to keep responses brief.

SMALL GROUP Make a two-column chart. Put "We Love" at the top of the left column and "We Love Not" at the top of the right.

ters. He wrote about loving to Christians living in a hostile world and awaiting the return of Christ. First Corinthians 13 was written to a divided community in which religious practices and spiritual gifts were at odds. Paul's efforts to unite these believers centered on love and a hope that the ability to love might govern all other gifts.

Paul offers more than a dozen facets of Christian love in this single chapter. He writes that a loving person is patient and kind, goes the distance, and willingly pays the price. He claims love's motive, integrity, hope, and steadfastness. But between the beginning of the fourth verse and the end of the seventh, Paul points a wagging finger at all that love is not!

The list of all that love is not is long! Pick your favorite adjectives to characterize a selfish "me first!" person who loves not. There's *jealous, arrogant, conceited, ill-mannered, rude, irritable, resentful,* and more! Then there are all the unpleasant activities associated with those who love not, such as *quarreling, boasting, loathing, gossiping,* and *scoffing.*

Loving is part of the character of a community. The behavior of the Corinthians limited the ability of their community to be faithful—to be a safe place where persons were concerned about the day-to-day well-being of one another and of their neighbor—the smallest unit of a community.

Leviticus 19 starts a list that includes the poor, daily laborers, the deaf and blind, and resident aliens. Jesus indiscriminately flung open the door so that all were included. We are called to be loving to anyone, including neighborhood outcasts and all those who are not naturally lovable—enemies, lepers, the wicked, criminals, strangers, the tormented, and the troubled.

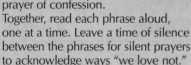

Love: Opening Your Heart to God and Others

LOVE MY ENEMIES?

Jamal: Christian followers don't retaliate. Period. End of discussion.

David: That's it? Hey, I'm a victim here. I'm well-acquainted with hatred, vengeance, and injury. I have the scars to prove it!

Amie: Not to react? That really runs against the grain. Getting even; doing it right back at them—it's a knee-jerk reaction. What happened to common sense?

David: It's not even reasonable. "Love your enemies, do good to those who hate you." Jesus needs to spend a little time in my reality.

Amie: I go home, get slapped around a little, and I'm not supposed to start swinging? Yeah, like if I just sit there and take it, it'll change somebody's life. He'll just think I've finally given in to his ways of "loving" me.

Jamal: No, you don't just sit there and take it. I didn't say, "Don't react." Walk out, but do no harm. Care about his well-being. Encourage him to get help.

David: Isn't that a bit much to ask?

Jamal: If we say we're brothers and sisters of Jesus, then we have to live with the Parent/child thing. If we are children of God and we've inherited any of God's holiness at all, then we have to love like God loves. What if God just loved those who love God? What if God turned away every time we turn away?

David: So God doesn't do what we do to God. That means I'm not supposed to mirror the hate and hurt of my enemies?

Amie: Mirror God. Be holy. Act with loving kindness and mercy. I think I get it, but how do I do it?

Love My Enemies
Read Luke 6:27-36. Answer Amie's question about how to do this. Is Amie loving as God loves if she remains in an abusive, unloving relationship? Explain. Talk about your own experience with your own enemies. How do you deal with your enemies? If you loved like Jesus, what would you do? How do you need to grow into this call to love?

Use a Bible commentary to look up this passage to get background about the cultural realities that lay behind these injunctions to love. What do all these instructions to turn the cheek, give your shirt, give away your goods, and lend without thought of repayment mean? What current examples can you identify? Is this good advice today or is it for idealists and chumps? Explain.

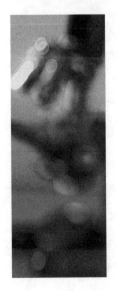

Dannika's Journal

Read John 7:53-8:11. This is also Dannikka's story. First interpret the biblical story. The scribes and Pharisees point to the woman's sin. Jesus points to the sin of the scribes and the Pharisees. None are innocent. All are charged. Jesus frees them all!

Form two break-out groups. One group will take on the experience of the scribes and the Pharisees. The other group will take on the life of the woman caught in adultery. Consider the following questions as you "see" the events unfold.

- What does Jesus do to bring about freedom?
- What does Jesus demand?
- Acquittal signals a new beginning. What's new in these lives? How might their living and doing be different?

Dannikka has lived this story. She's been freed by Christ's sacrifice—God's steadfast love and mercy. She lives in love by the grace and power of the Holy Spirit. You've been forgiven! So what's new? How do you claim the freedom Christ offers you? How has your living and doing changed?

Use this story to initiate a discussion or substitute an experience of liberation and grace of your own.

DANNIKKA'S JOURNAL

Jesus, I am she. Now what?
I know you are. Wait.
What are you writing?
Shhh . . .
"I have come not to condemn—"
Let any among you who is without sin cast the first stone.
"—but to save."
Where are they?
They've gone.
No stones?
None.
None from me either.
But I'm guilty. I—
Don't try to defend yourself. There is no need. Love knows. Love sent me to bring grace upon grace.
Grace upon grace?
Yes. I have come to save you, to give you life.
Life? I don't have to die?
No! You are a child of Love, hallowed and holy. Trust Love now and live!
I have sinned against the Law and jeopardized the ones I love.
You are given life by the grace of Love. You are free, forgiven, reconciled, and saved by Love's mercy. Go, live. Love and sin no more.
I am overwhelmed by such a deep love. What a treasure! Words cannot express my gratitude. All I can do is live. Let me live as one who delivers grace and mercy from the heart. Let me live as one who is quick to forgive and slow to condemn, because her life has been spared. Let me be a blessing as I live in your love.

COMMUNITY LIVE!

Skirmish in the Ranks

Jesus acknowledged the possibility of antagonism, friction, and discord in a faith community. What begins as a personal offense can quickly escalate and overwhelm a whole church. Jesus prescribes action to resolve disputes, seek justice, save the sinner, and restore community.

The aggrieved takes the initiative, seeks out the offender, and points out the problem. This is the first turning point. If the dispute is resolved, there is reason for rejoicing. If not, then others (not witnesses) must be brought to the table to help mediate. Here's the second turning point. If justice wins out, then celebrate! If not, then the controversy becomes a matter of concern for the whole body.

The effect of unreconciled dispute in the congregation is great. Greater still is the power of an "out-of-court settlement" negotiated in a spirit of love and forgiveness. This radical caring, coupled with the recognition of Christ in the midst of community, strengthens the whole church.

Justis

Justis's "hate me/hurt me" stuff had gotten way out of hand the past couple of weeks. None of us had seen him eat for days. He was drunk a lot, drinking on top of his anti-panic attack drugs. Last Tuesday, in a fit of rage, he pulled a knife on himself. That's when we saw the other cuts and marks of self-inflicted mutilation.

Justis claimed we were all ganging up on him, that we were to blame for all his trouble. It was our standards that he couldn't live up to. It was all our fault.

DISCUSS

Skirmish
The community of faith is so interconnected that the offense of one can act upon the whole body. Take a moment to gather your knowledge of church disputes. Together develop a church argument scenario or examine the profile of a common church conflict experience.

Identify the facts of the case. Compare the actions taken to moderate justice and reconciliation with those outlined by Jesus. Evaluate the outcome of the action along a continuum of resolution. All efforts failed? What if the accused is as an enemy or sinner? What are the next salvation steps?

Now read Matthew 18:15-21 as a model for resolving community conflict. How does it compare to the methods you have used elsewhere? to methods that have worked or not worked?

CASE STUDY

Justis
Use Justis's story or one from your own experience to look into how the community rallies, loves, and supports, especially when the object of that support doesn't make it easy. What happened to Justis in the space between his pain and his hope? How might Justis's communities be helping to carry his burdens and uphold him? How might the community of faith support Justis during treatment and in recovery?

We called a couple of his colleagues, his mom, and our minister and got him admitted to the hospital. He was released yesterday afternoon on a 24-hour pass so he could care for personal business.

Our pastor incorporated a service of healing into this morning's worship liturgy. The whole congregation gathered around Justis. We prayed for him, laid hands on him, and anointed him.

A bunch of us got him back to the hospital earlier this afternoon. Now I'm starting to wonder how it will be when he's able to come home to stay.

COME AND BELONG

The party is planned. The host has made the guest list and sent the invitations. It's a bad night—folks are busy and they cannot come. They give notice and excuses. More folks are invited. After all, the host has a contract with the caterer and the musicians; there might as well be a party!

The new guest list includes faces from the neighborhood. At this neighborhood block party, there are no strings attached; no obligatory claims, favors, or conditions; no expectation of a reciprocal invitation. It's not a client meeting, a chance to schmooze and impress or finagle a favor. Everybody sits down together and shares food and fellowship. The host welcomes them with affection, offers them the customary arrival amenities and courtesies, and tends to their comfort. The host extends hospitality to the guests.

Hospitality is that great concern and care shown as we receive our neighbors in love. It embraces an attitude of humility that is reflected in a willingness to receive whatever a guest might have to offer by his or her pres-

Come and Belong
Read Luke 14:12-24.
Jesus speaks first to his Pharisee host about being a host. What is the significance of sharing life and bread with those who cannot return the invitation? What is the difference between inviting folks from the neighborhood to the table and just finding a way to feed them? What does the guest list tell us about God's love? our love? about God's neighborhood? our communities?

A comment from a dinner guest inspires Jesus to tell a story. It looks like maybe the Pharisee's guests were not included on the list of neighbors seated at table in Jesus' story. What is the point of the story for the Pharisee's guests? for us?

Love: Opening Your Heart to God and Others

ence. Such generosity is not earned by a guest or extended out of a position of superiority, but given simply out of a desire to receive the blessings of those led by Christ to be in our midst. Out of the grace and wisdom of hospitality comes action that welcomes.

On one occasion, Jesus was the guest in the home of a Pharisee. The host and guest were reclining in the courtyard and dining together, when an uninvited woman approached Jesus. She was a sinner and a harlot. Out of her love and gratitude, she washed Jesus' feet, dried them with her hair, kissed his feet, and anointed them. The one whose sins were many offered hospitality. How ironic! The woman's actions of hospitality embarrassed and insulted the host. Jesus received the woman's gestures of hospitality and then offered his own graciousness to her. Jesus forgave the woman, saved her, restored her, and freed her. Jesus acted in the character of God the host.

Read Luke 7:36-50. Look for both specific and implicit gestures of hospitality. Make a list.

Pick up your journal or sit with a couple of group members you trust. Tell about a time in your life when you were a guest in God's presence and experienced God's gestures of hospitality. How were you welcomed by God? How did you receive God's actions? How did you feel?

We host our neighbors as guests of God. What of your experience as God's guest can you translate into actions as a host?

GROWING IN LOVE

You are a child of God. You know yourself to be in God's love. This love includes those whom God has created in every conceivable community connection.

It takes a lifetime to grow in love. We love our neighbor until the one next door can't speak our language or gets arrested for drug trafficking. We can feed the hungry so long as it is not at our own table. We do our part to settle things between our neighbors until we are the ones wronged and our lawyers advise that we file suit. We seek fairness unless it cuts into our profits. We support healing and those in recovery so long as they don't smoke in our church building. This "love" lasts only until we decide not to love.

Growing in Love
Look at the contrasts in how we love and the point at which we often fail to love. Do you find these contrasts true for you? for most of the people you know? Or are they unusual for you? for others you know?

What is the point at which you decide not to love? When is the loving gesture too hard to make? What is the difference between "tough love" (which fails to bail out someone who needs to accept his or her own responsibilities and consequences) and failing to love (because it's too inconvenient, or difficult)?

Table Manners

You and some of your friends agree to meet at the local coffeehouse after being scattered to the wind for more than a few days. The first person to arrive picks a booth and sits down. A couple of friends sit down, another person comes, and then one more. The last one pulls up a chair in the aisle at the end of the booth and sits down. Management comes through, mumbles something about fire code, and pulls the chair out from under the late arrival. He's forced to occupy the adjacent booth, sit on his knees, and hang over the back of the seat to try to keep up with the conversation. The food comes and suddenly someone notices that Jessica's missing and wonders if she got the word.

Your family makes holiday meal reservations at a fine restaurant. It is a four-generation gathering. As your family is invited to be seated, the maitre d' informs you that they were not able to honor your request to seat everyone around the same table.

Jesus ate with everyone. Whether it was dinner at the home of a tax collector or a lunch shared by a crowd on a hillside, Jesus was known for his table fellowship. He was constantly tested and challenged because of his full acceptance of all those gathered at table with him. Jesus was identified, tried, and crucified—in part because of his "table manners."

At Christ's table we get told who we are!

We learn and develop our table customs around a big, big table of love. Then, we become known by our own distinctive table manners.

HOW YOU LOVE EACH OTHER

This session will look at the desire, capacity, promises, and threats of intimate and sacramental love.

VOICES OF INTIMACY

Thad: I'd say I "give up" or "give in" to love. I tested Sarah for a long time. I really needed to be able to trust her before we got too serious. Promising to love is so risky. Sex is so complicated. Trying to get close has made for some of the worst moments in my life!

Nicole: Ever since we met, I've done everything with Marci in mind. I'll call her and check in. I spend all of my time away from work with her. It's like I'm always with her. My life is Marci's life.

Lani: Can I say sex is holy? When Ty touches me it's like God showing me a me who is truly lovely, who can love and give.

Lisha: When I met Derik I knew I finally found the one I would love. I'm not sure I can explain. It's just that some fire got lit, some essential something that was lost got found, and I heard some new harmony that I had never heard before. He aroused such a longing in me. I knew that I would not be complete without Derik.

Conversations about intimacy can be difficult for some persons. No one should feel obligated to reveal what is shared intimately or privately with another person. You may choose to work through this material with your partner or someone else you trust. If you are uncomfortable in this environment, postpone exploring these topics until you are in a more private setting.

Greet each other. Welcome and identify any newcomers. Invite each other to offer a brief "love grown since last we met" update. Ask for specific support and prayers and honor requests for prayer and nurturing.

Voices

Thad, Nicole, and Lisha talk about intimate love. Reflect on the portrayals. Which matches best with your own experience of intimacy? How would you describe intimate love?

Sacrament

SMALL GROUP

Familiar actions, certain places, endearing words and songs, and ordinary things from our real lives help us know more about God. Describe how you have experienced God's sacramental grace in the context of an intimate relationship.

L O O K CLOSER

Passionate Affection

Read Song of Solomon 4:1-7, 8-15. In verses 1-7, the woman speaks of her lover; the only place in Scripture where a man's masculinity and male beauty are extolled from a female point of view. In verses 8-15, the young man replies. Read each gender's respective verses aloud.

Listen for the possessive, delightful, sexual, and romantic preoccupation of the lovers. See how they refer to each other in terms of endearment preceded by the first person singular possessive pronoun "my." Notice how the lovers offer similar praise to describe sensuality and beauty. Search for expressions of intimacy that suggest mutuality.

INTIMACY AS SACRAMENT

Sacraments connect us with God's grace. A sacramental action is an outward and visible sign that defines the sacred or holy. God moves through our actions, places, words, things, and relationships so that we can see God's goodness and love. God uses our day-to-day lives to make what is invisible, visible. Thanks to God's grace, all of life is potentially sacramental.

Love acted out in the context of an intimate relationship is sacramental. The passionate affection aroused by a lover's voice or touch can point beyond genital sex to God's creative energy. The power of deep love to reveal true value or worth, to heal, or to forgive can witness to the reality of God's grace and presence. When we choose to love another and pledge our faithfulness, it can remind us of our covenant with God. To turn away from our own self-centeredness and give ourselves to another can make God's sacrificial love for us more than just rhetoric. We give thanks for God's sacramental grace.

PASSIONATE AFFECTION

Passionate affection can be aroused by the sound of another's voice or passing touch. This sensuality and longing honors the human need and desire to be loved, to engage in an open and tender relationship, and experience the joy of love. This attraction ensures that the "it is good" unity and relationship in creation will prevail over human isolation and loneliness.

For lovers and partners, it's not just the sound of a voice that attracts. There's a private language—sometimes daring, often tender, always open, and at times, necessarily frank. It is discovered, developed, and nurtured in mutual devotion and exclusive affection.

As we read the Song of Solomon (Song of Songs), we eavesdrop on an intimate dialogue between a man and a woman who seek to cultivate, nurture, safeguard, and cherish one another. The lovers use pet names and coded, metaphoric speech to be mindful and attentive to each other. Their language reflects the push and pull of commitment, the dreams and fantasies of passion, and the dangers and demands of love fulfilled.

Sexual Intimacy

The lovers continue their sensual and poetic exchanges. The true beauty of love has been awakened! By the end of the seventh chapter (Song of Solomon 7:10-12), the woman is identifying herself by the love she feels for her "prince" (6:12). She claims *his* desire for her. The beloved promises her love boldly and declares her intention to give herself to him.

Sex is a generous way to express affection and love. Genital sex embraces the yearning, vulnerability, and dependence of intimacy, plus all its obstacles and frustrations. The physical pleasures of human intimacy and love can hint at God's passionate affection for us and point us toward spiritual intimacy with God.

Sexual sharing changes intimacy. Sex begs trust, seeks belonging, and sacrifices autonomy. It is risky, even as it is offered in the context of mutuality, respect, and love. Lovemaking that "fits" beckons us to link our lives in other ways.

Think about your daily language with others, especially with those to whom you are the most intimate. How often do you affirm them? compliment them? support them? How often is your language less soft or loving than it could be for the situation? Is there any pattern you might want to change?

SMALL GROUP

Sexual Intimacy Pick up your journal or sit with your partner or a couple of group members you trust. Write your own love poetry. Try to employ contemporary metaphors and your own personal language of love to speak of intimacy. If you wish, use the Scripture as a model.

How does it feel to read such sensuous poetry in the Bible as found in Song of Solomon? Scholars debate about whether the language is a metaphor of God's love for Israel or of Christ's love for the church. On the surface it's just love poetry, extolling the physical appearance and pleasure the young man and woman give each other.

Lani and Ty (on page 59) expressed their affection and love sexually. In pairs, talk about what you regard as intimate sexual expression (which can be physical without being coital). Reflect on the sexual expression of affection and love in your own experience. Do you find sex to be holy? In your own sexual expressions of love what promises were made? What questions were asked? How has sexuality opened your heart? How has it informed your understanding of God's passionate love for you? How has sex drawn you closer to God?

CASE STUDY

Power of Love

Lisha suggests that a new "us" was born out of her intimate love with Derik. Speculate about how Lisha and Derik might have recognized and nurtured this growing love. What's the significance of the new "(1+1) > 2 us?" How might their friends and families have experienced this new relationship? What connections might be made between Lisha and Derik's intimate love and God's abiding love?

DISCUSS

If you are in a new relationship, what signs do you look for that tell you that there may be more than just friendship? If you are in a more developed relationship, what elements of that "first love" do you strive to keep? What, if any, have you lost? Discuss.

POWER OF LOVE

When a deep and abiding love can be expressed, it does a body, mind, and heart good! Intimacy has the capacity to reveal loveliness, offer grace, promote healing, and extend forgiveness. It can move us beyond our own self-centeredness to shared hopes and mutual obligations. Such enduring love nurtures and creates newness.

Lisha

I had my degree in one hand and a new job contract in the other. All the pieces of my life were in place and everything was just right. One of my friends brought Derik to the coffeehouse where we met every Monday night. He fit in with everybody so well. I hardly even noticed how close we were getting. Then Derik and I became "us"—not just a "merger" or the sum of some good "synergy"—but something altogether new. This new "us" made it possible to give and love and care for each other in ways neither of "us" had known before. Together we had much more to offer all our other relationships.

An Entry From Amie's Journal

I try to trust, but it's just too much of a stretch. It's just too impossible. I have too many strikes against me. Why would anybody want to love me? I can't even begin to believe the promises of intimacy and love. Mary, the mother of Jesus, said "Yes!" and trusted. Sarah, Abraham's wife, laughed and doubted, and she had a long-desired child. God made good on both impossible promises. The human answer didn't seem to make any difference at all. A child was born to a virgin and to an old woman. God acted anyway.

While the possibility of an intimate relationship seems so hopeless to me right now, it pales in comparison to the impossibility that God made possible for Sarah. God's promise was more powerful than Sarah's doubt. What does that mean for me and the promise of love?

Here I am, God, stewing in impossibility. Though it doesn't seem to make any difference, I want to trust the promises of love. By your grace and in your mercy, trade my hopelessness, doubt, fear, and disbelief for trust. Make me a witness to love's power according to your promises.

DISCUSS

How have you experienced the promises of intimacy and love in your own life? Talk about times when you've seen love override feelings of hopelessness, doubt, fear, and disbelief. What about the possibility in impossibility? Answer Amie's question for yourself: Why would someone love you? (There are lots of reasons!) Then try to claim God's power to open your own heart to the promises of love.

CHOSEN LOVE

The people of Israel were chosen by God to be a treasured possession. God willingly chose love and acted out *hesed*, and that love found a home in covenant and commitment.

Nicole

I met Marci and decided that she was someone that I could actually trust. Nobody has known me like this since I was a child. We love and treasure each other. We have chosen to know, and to be known by, each other. We respect each other and risk vulnerability together. We have an honest and open relationship. Everything about our relationship is negotiated.

Ruth's *Hesed*

Ruth's decision to love Naomi took her into a foreign country with little more than hand-to-mouth sustenance (Ruth 1). Boaz, a distant male relative, provided help and support for the two women (Ruth 2). Naomi planned for Ruth to approach Boaz

CASE STUDY 2

Chosen Love
Use the example of Nicole and Marci or an experience of your own to examine how we choose to navigate in our relationships. Choosing, deciding, and negotiating may seem like sterile language to use in the context of an intimate and loving relationship. But deciding how we are to be known in a relationship is part of loving and living. How might Nicole and Marci define intimacy? What ways of loving may have been mutually negotiated in respect to this definition? How much are you willing to bend and accommodate in your own relationships? What do you do when the "give and take" seems out of balance?

Read Ruth 3–4.
Outline Naomi's plan in detail. Identify junctions in the plan according to the choice to be made and the character who must choose. Discuss the actions of all three characters. What faithful ways of expressing love and intimacy are demonstrated in this story? Look for outward and visible signs of the inward and spiritual grace of God's love.

Electing to Commit
The lovers in the Song of Solomon choose to set a seal on their relationship (Song of Solomon 8:6). What contributes to the decision to marry or to somehow seal a relationship? What actions make and keep the commitment firm? How are promises gone awry reconciled? What do we do when the covenant fails?

Threats
Examine one or more of theses Scriptures: 2 Samuel 11:1-27; 13:1-22; Judges 19:16-30. You may choose to spend time with the Scripture independently, in pairs, or in break-out groups. What happened? Who was responsible and who acknowledged responsibility?

and pursue the security of marriage. Ruth complied and cooperated with the plan, choosing to stand steadfast and faithful as Naomi saw to their future.

Ruth was not responsible for keeping the name and sustaining the lineage of her deceased husband. Boaz was under no moral or legal obligation to marry Ruth. Ruth and Boaz chose to love, and their intimacy was grounded in the faithful kindness and loyalty of *hesed* (Ruth 3–4).

Electing to Commit

The actions and promises of intimate love need a protected place to grow. For many, that place is within the commitment of marriage. As a legal contract, marriage is legislated. As a religious covenant, marriage is pledged. The commitments of marriage—to give and receive, to be loyal and faithful for life—provide a protective framework that helps intimacy to flourish.

Marriage is not a part of every life. For some, marriage may not be an appropriate way to recognize the affection, compassion, and respect that characterizes their relationship. But without an oath, covenant, or commitment to cherish, the risk to intimacy is greater.

THREATS TO INTIMACY

Intimacy is threatened by self-centered power and induced fear. Arrogant misuse of power creates too much closeness for intimacy. Fear creates too much distance for intimacy. Lust, desire, anger, anxiety, and grief are all carried out as self-indulgent and coercive actions in adultery, rape, and domestic violence.

Adultery. King David acted swiftly. He sent for Bathsheba, the object of his desire. She came, laid, and left, but later announced, "I am pregnant." Those three words triggered a cover-up that ended in murder (2 Samuel 11:1-27).

Rape. Amnon loved Tamar. His passion and craving for sex collided head-on with what was tolerated. Tamar resisted, but in an act of unprincipled egocentrism, Amnon forcibly oppressed, raped, and humiliated Tamar (2 Samuel 13:1-22).

Domestic Violence. A dispensable female is sacrificed in a grotesque perversion of hospitality. The atrocity of a nameless concubine's repeated rape and abuse strikes no chords of guilt, shame, or remorse in the heart of the self-absorbed Levite (Judges 19:16-28); he is only angry that the mob killed her (19:29-30).

Use these questions as discussion starters on the Scriptures to examine threats to intimacy. What appear to be the human feelings or traits that motivate the self-seeking actions of the main character? Specify the particulars of each compelling action and relationship. What happens to hasten the threat? How is the threat finally realized? What self-preservation cover-up tactics (scapegoating, rationalizing, silencing, or romanticizing) are put to use to absolve the injustice?

BEYOND ONE'S SELF

Paul's letter to the Ephesians was written at a time when companionship in marriage was improbable. Women had no legal status, husbands easily exercised their right to divorce, and wives reckoned their lives through their husbands. Against this backdrop, Paul proposed a new and radical framework for mutuality in relationships (Ephesians 5:21-33).

Paul's basic covenant of mutual responsibility and accountability has the capacity to protect and preserve all intimate and loving relationships. The framework calls for a type of unity that, in day-to-day living, reflects the union of Christ and the church. Intimacy is marked by loving, revering, understanding, giving, cherishing, building up, and bringing out the best in one another.

Beyond One's Self
Read Ephesians 5:21-33 and use a Bible commentary to further examine this passage and its context. How is this notion of equal relationship between husband and wife a radical one for its day? for now?

LOOK CLOSER

It is realized when each self gives in and finds their own loving self as they love another. Intimacy says "I will" to a sacrificial, caring, and unbreakable love.

Thad

Sarah and I really had to choose what sort of relationship we wanted. We're both strong Christians, so we try to be with each other as Christ is with us. Some of the decisions we are making about our household will be different than Paul's counsel, but still, each of us will carry specific duties, responsibilities, and authorities. We've been challenged to live by the phrase, "Which one of you will love the most?" When we marry, we will pledge to offer all that we are and all that we have in devotion to one another and to Jesus Christ.

GROWING IN LOVE

You are a child of God. You know yourself to be in God's love. It takes a lifetime to grow in love. We crave intimacy, but are too selfish to give ourselves to another. We use terms of endearment as weapons. We try too hard to earn another person's love. Desire turns into demand that distances us. Fear hijacks our yearning for physical, emotional, and spiritual closeness and we end up isolated and lonely. In one breath we promise to love and be faithful, and in the next we limit and qualify the conditions of intimacy.

Jesus modeled how to love intimately and sacramentally—how to recognize the presence of God in ourselves, how to be reminded of the holy in other persons, and how to hint at God's affection in every interaction.

ABIDE IN LOVE

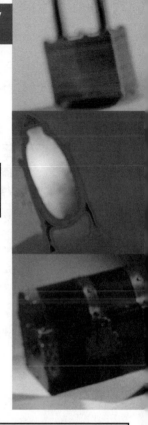

> This session will claim love as an acting and doing verb that enhances and builds up the person and the community.

GETTING STARTED

"Don't talk about love; show me!" We identify a lot of things as love (even though some of them really aren't). We speak of feelings, including affection, infatuation, and lust in our casual definition of love as well as attitudes of devotion, allegiance, and duty. Are these really love?

LEE

God's love makes all other love possible. Love is how God *is* with us, not just how God *feels* about us. We know love and therefore we know God. But God loves first, then we love. In this mutual love, God abides with us; that is, God stays close so we can continue to love.

In fact, Christians believe that we can't *do* love without God because it comes from God first. The caring question—"Me first or you first?"—is moot, unless we know God's love. Everything that God does is loving, even if we don't realize or understand it at the time.

It's like a May Pole dance. God is the pole and love is the ribbons. We take the ribbons in hand and do a dance that entwines us

START Greet each other. Welcome and identify any newcomers. Invite each other to offer a brief "love grown since last we met" update. Feel free to ask for specific support and prayers. Be ready to honor requests for prayer and nurturing.

DISCUSS

Lee
Read about God's love in 1 John 4:7-16. Try to develop an analogy, simile, metaphor, image, or symbol that meaningfully interprets God's indicative love. Does the May Pole metaphor work for you? How would you explain or define love?

and our neighbors with God's love. Don't like the May Pole analogy? How would you explain love?

OUR LOVE; GOD'S LOVE

Human love is imperative. We are children of God and created to love. We are disposed to loving and we ought to love, but we still have to choose to love. We can also choose death, darkness, and hate. We are capable of doing horrible things. As Christians, we can affirm that God loves us even when we sin, not that God's love excuses the sin. In a superlative act of love, Jesus Christ laid down his life for love—a love that helps us take responsibility and admit wrong; a love that unlocks forgiveness and promises new life.

This new life is based on action, though, and not just talk or feelings. Love only in word or speech is not really love at all. Our love is to be a visible reminder of God's love, which is revealed to others by acts of caring. We are known as the children of God because we love actively. Jesus actively and willingly laid down his life for us; something we are unlikely to be called to do for another. More often, it is in simple acts of compassion that we show our love. God makes our love a reality.

A Prayer From Dannikka's Journal

God, I know your love. Your grace has taken hold of my heart. Your love has changed me from the inside out. You have planted love deep within me. You call me beloved, and I am. I have received your love and the call to love. I have a whole life ahead of me, a whole life to love.

Our Love, God's Love
Read 1 John 3:1-11. What does it mean to you to be a child of God? What is sin? (First, it is willful rebellion against and separation from God; next we also think of it as specific actions or attitudes that are contrary to God's love and will.) What does being a child of God have to do with love and sin?

SMALL GROUP

Dannika's Journal
Pick up your journal or sit with a trusted friend or two for prayer. Trust the power of prayer in combination with everyday actions of love. Claim God's indicative love. Recognize your imperative call to choose and fulfill a life of love. Acknowledge your life in the world; not alone against the world, but in the world with God's mercy and grace. Offer your heart to God. Ask God for all that you need to meet human need in truth and action. Close this time of prayer by reading 1 John 3:23-24 and singing a song of praise.

Keep me in your loving arms; keep hold of my actions; let me radiate the light of your love. Meet me and be present with me. Meet me with the gifts and power of the Spirit. Meet me with your grace and mercy. Meet me in the places and spaces, in the eyes and hands, and in the feet and hearts of others who share your love. Let me love as one who is loved. Amen.

PERFECTING LOVE

You are a child of God. You know yourself to be in God's love. You choose love and recognize that God makes love happen. You trust the mutual and reciprocal abiding that is promised by the Spirit.

It takes a lifetime to grow in love. We can never reach the limit of our ability to love. God's love is limitless; how could our love be any other way? We will really never "arrive," but by grace we keep moving toward God. (Thanks be to God!) The goal is bold and confident action, a love that goes out to others and forgets self; a perfect love that abandons self-interest and self-concern and directs all our day-to-day actions. Along the way to our goal of perfect love, we may encounter a number of imperfect ways to love. In fact, these imperfections may not really be love at all.

A Slave's "Love"

A slave has no rights; he or she is expected to submit, not reason. The incentive to do is founded in fear. It's tough to love if you are always looking over your shoulder in fear. Fear cripples us. It pushes us to "love" out of a legalistic duty that requires us to live up to some (usually) impossible or unloving standard of perfection or performance.

Perfecting Love
In "popcorn" style, quickly toss out suggestions on how to know when love has "arrived."

Next, suggest (or sing) music lyrics that describe or define "perfected love" or decry imperfect love. What portrait of love emerges?

Read 1 John 4:16b-19. Pick up each of the phrases in these verses and examine them one at a time. What is the place of fear in the context of love? If fear is a part of an intimate relationship with anyone, including God, can it be truly loving? Explain. Accept the invitation to take up residence in a life of love. What is promised? How does God's love and Christ's sacrifice alleviate the fear and free us to grow in love?

Abide in Love

The love required of a "slave" often hides behind the facade, "If you really loved me, you would—." But this is manipulation or domination, not love. It requests or demands "love" that is based on fear from non-compliance. The Book of First John declares that there is no room in love for fear (4:18).

A Hireling's Love

A hired hand acts out of a desire to please or earn a reward. A hireling only acquires necessary information, such as who needs to be kept happy and how much effort it will take. A hired hand just does the job and collects the pay. Personal well-being is the hireling's primary concern.

Perhaps you know someone who sees a need in another and works to meet it with the expectation of affection, devotion, or love in return. Perhaps you know of someone who always sucks up to the boss to show allegiance. Perhaps you know someone who doesn't challenge unhealthy behavior in another because that behavior is somehow rewarding to the codependent one. These persons are like hirelings who want to gain allegiance or promote their own self-interest, but is this really love? God's love cannot be earned; it was given before we could offer any love in return. To grow in love is to willingly go above and beyond the call of duty. Loving is a disposition that chooses to love—a whole way of sensing, understanding, and being.

A Friend's Love

Friends, unlike the slave or hireling, embrace the unity and mutuality that make love possible. Friends lower the barriers and reveal the needs between them so they can love each other freely, with joy.

As Jesus' hour of Passion approached, the status of the disciples was changed from follower to friend (John 15:9-17). They were called friends because Jesus had kept nothing about God from them; they were intimately engaged in relationship with God. As friends of Jesus, they shared the power to forgive, the ability to initiate acceptance, and the love to embrace the unlovely and unlovable.

BIBLE

Read John 15:9-17. How does Jesus describe a friend in this passage? What does it mean to be this kind of friend? Do you have any friends like this?

Amie

Everybody was home the other night and we really cooked. Nobody needed to be off anywhere and we sat around the table for hours. That's when I trusted Jamal, David, and the others with the whole "growing-up-at-my-house" story.

At first, I thought maybe I was doing it just for me, but that's not how it was received! There was no "poor Amie" stuff, no patronizing sympathy. My friends offered dignity and respect, care and compassion—love.

We're all on the same page now. Jamal and the others are so grateful for my trust. There's a certain joy in the house. We're in a new place; we really treasure and love each other.

CASE STUDY

Amie
Amie claimed that Jamal, David, and the others in the apartment were friends. How was that perception confirmed? What actions made dignity and respect, care, and compassion known to Amie? What fosters love in this household? What fosters love in your household?

LOVE IS A VERB

Amie's friends do not treat her like a slave or a hireling. They do not require her to do or be someone who lives up to their particular expectations; they love her for who she is, and that love is shown in action by their acceptance.

As Christians we are called to love actively, unconditionally, and freely to promote

LOOK CLOSER

Love Is a Verb
To act in love is at least two thousand years old! Grab a concordance and make a list of Scripture references that catch Jesus acting in love. Then, make another list of New Testament references that admonish us to do the same.
Choose a verse or two that means something to you and commit them to memory.

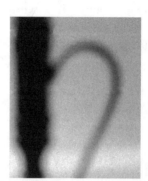

the well-being of persons, to act for the good of others, and to do no harm. When we open ourselves to the unselfish opportunities to love, we become better able to identify with others in their pain and their victories. We become more like Jesus, wholly devoted to the helpless and less than faithful to powers, principalities, and "the way we've always done it."

Biblical Studies 101: Love in Action
First John 3:16-18 is a concise reminder that love is not found first in "word or speech," but in "truth and action." It asks the very practical question: How does God's love abide in any-one who has the world's goods and sees a brother or sister in need and yet refuses to help?
How, indeed? John knew then what we know now. To use a modern metaphor, talk is cheap. John challenged the Christian community to put their money where their mouth was. If we as Christians are content to look on while our brothers and sisters suffer, we show no evidence of the Christ we claim.

Discern and Decide

Love is not just a flurry of "nice" activity here and there; it takes some discernment. Faithful doers will stop to think about what they feel they need to do. Discernment keeps our faith close to our routine decision-making and helps us decide if what we are doing is "full of self" or "full of God." It is based on the belief that God still speaks today to those who have ears to hear. Those who pause in their activity to discern claim that there is a Guide who is present to lead them closer to Christ, closer to one another, and closer to the world God wills. Discernment means sifting out the urgings of the Holy Spirit from other promises, voices, impulses, and motivations that would lead us otherwise.

Do With Humility

Having made a decision to put our love to work, we do so with humility. The original Greek *tapeinophrosune* refers to one who is long-suffering, lowly, and meek. Humility has no trouble believing that God loves and that the worth of all persons comes from God. Humility puts us all in the same boat! It has the ability to see that all people are equally valuable in God's eyes. It recognizes our flaws as easily as we see the faults of others.

Humility has no time for judgment or scorn. It doesn't jostle for power or need to be "right." Humility stands in opposition to all that fuels "-isms," pride, and neglect. It frees doers to claim the realities of the human condition and tend to real needs.

Loving Humbly

BIBLE

Loving Humbly
Read Ephesians 4:1-7. Look at the headlines in a local newspaper or check the news services on the internet. Connect the actions of the Scripture with the lead stories. Create an inventory of distinct actions that either *refuse* or *offer* in response to the suffering and affliction reported in the news. What gifts did persons bring to these actions? What gifts do you bring?

Biblical Studies 101: Loving Humbly

Paul, in Ephesians 4:1-7, puts humility in context with other qualities of Christian living and doing. Authentic humility, gentleness, patience, and love also apply to the person who puts love in action. Doers are not to bear guilt for what is left undone. They start small and learn to take up specific and appropriate tasks and assume positions that either refuse to harm or offer help. We aren't perfect. We can't do it all, but each is apportioned particular gifts according to God's grace, and in the exercise of these gifts, we put love to work. In all that we do, we must be gentle, patient, and loving with ourselves.

DO IT!

All who take upon themselves the name of Christ are called to love and be doers

Abide in Love

Do It!

As a group discern, decide, plan, and act in love by "preparing a table before your enemies" (Psalm 23:5). Begin by asking one another what God is guiding your group to do in the face of this challenge. What is the nature of the fear or dispute? Whose voices need to be heard? How many ways can a table that seeks justice, extends forgiveness, and offers new life be set? Weigh your options carefully and choose one to do.

Ask the following questions: Is this action "full of God" or "full of self"? What are three important things about the chosen option? What are the concerns? How can this concern become a positive value in the long run? What are the implementing steps? Who will be responsible? How might it be accomplished? When will it be done? How practical and realistic are the implementing steps? How is energy being committed to this action?

Commission one another to live and love in the fullness of God. Use this prayer provided or create one that reflects your group's experience and life together.

Conclude this prayer with a song of commitment or a praise chorus. Offer one another signs of Christian love.

according to the example of Christ. Doers let their actions witness to the steadfast love of God. Doers are equipped with:

- Plenty of love. We can act in the interest of our own well-being and that of friends, family, neighbors we can't call by name, and our most intimate relationships.
- Compassion and the means by which to give it real meaning.
- Humility and a gentle heart.
- Patience.
- Hands that do, even when the head doesn't understand why.
- Faith and trust that surrender and give in, according to the Spirit.

GOING FORTH

Sit down in the presence of one another to pray. Call each other by name and pray that each be firmly rooted and grounded in love. Ask for God's wisdom to cultivate all that fosters love and God's will to show love. Pray for the mind of Christ. Ask that the Spirit's power help fight all that stands in the way of loving.

Pray: "God, we choose love! We love with compassion, humility, a gentle heart, and patience. We do with heads and hearts that seek your will and hands that trust. Make our love known in all we do. Let our love be a witness to your way in the world. Amen."

CASE STUDIES

Getting Started

Use any of these cases in place of or in addition to the cases in the sessions as a means of stimulating discussion.

Drina

This woman is a religious icon. In her, you can see the image of God. Her life offers a wide glimpse of God's love. Once upon a time, not quite thirty years ago, she was born into a wealthy Roman Catholic family. Now Drina lives in a three-room, cardboard home with a dirt floor and no electricity. She is the "soul" of the neighborhood.

She claims that she is called to "shout the gospel" with her life. She lives with the poor to witness to the hope that is part of her own neighbors' struggle. She is present to them, outrageously vulnerable, and extremely hospitable. To watch her live is to see God love.

- What does Drina mean when she claims a call to "shout the gospel" with her life?
- If you spent a day with Drina, what might you see her do?
- What Scripture passages and images does she embody?
- What qualities of love does Drina embrace that you would like to grow?

Lino

I live in a mid-size city with distinctive ethnic neighborhoods. My parents and their siblings came here from Cuba just before I was born.

About a year ago, I was approached to run for office in city government. One of the main campaign issues is education. The candidates are claiming it as an intergenerational agenda, capable of uniting the community. I've been doing a lot of listening, and I'm not so sure.

In this precinct, my generation is multi-ethnic and primarily Hispanic. The older generation is Anglo. The generations agree on the importance of education but have very different opinions about the cause of the present concerns and the potential solutions. My generation tends to blame a lack of economic resources for education's problems. The older adults blame individuals for their lack of success in the system. My peers seem to lobby harder for prevention programs while the older citizens would rather react as specific needs surface. Of course, we can't talk about education without debating the English-only issue.

Right now, I have more questions than answers. The election is less than 60 days away.

- What does community concern look like? Is this an issue of how well we love one another?
- Does the neighborhood desire unity?
- How important is community for the children?
- What if the constituencies of the community fail to care for the well-being of one another?
- Can differences be accommodated within systems, or can unity in diversity only be realized if new community is created?

Trey

Our affair was extra-marital. The attraction was almost instant. Our actions, special places, and secret language nurtured and kept our bond of passion secure for quite some time. Eventually the relationship turned ugly on us. Somehow in the midst of our anger, regret, accusations, and hate, we chose to care. We agreed not to further jeopardize our families or careers. We made a pact not to hurt each other any more. Some crazy kind of loving, huh?

- What faithful ways of expressing love are evidenced in this relationship? Does their mutual agreement to break up mitigate what they did to begin with?
- Does Trey's experience witness to the grace of God's love? Explain.

Tasha

I guess there's a misfit in every clan. Dillon is the one who doesn't quite fit-in; the one who has typically tarnished our extended family's image. Dillon is a lot younger than I am, but I remember that school was never the right place for him. He married young and had a couple of kids who were born with some major health problems. He had a job most of the time, but never stayed at any one job long enough to get benefits or to see a pay raise. Recently, I heard he had divorced and that he is trying to get through trade school. I guess he has a new squeeze and a child by her.

My cousins and I are really not close at all. None of this would have much of an impact on us at all if our folks weren't so concerned about Grandpa. Grandpa deals with an even hand and a generous heart. Some say that Dillon is conning Grandpa. I really don't know if Dillon gets any kind of support from anybody, but I do know Grandpa. I'd say he's trying to love Dillon home.

- Introduce Dillon into the experience of the youngest son in Luke 15. How are the circumstances similar? different?
- What could happen if patience, forgiveness, mercy, and grace could make a way into this story?
- What if Dillon is conning Grandpa? Then what? How else might Grandpa show his love?
- How is God in, with, under, and behind the actions of this family?

Rachelle

I called off our wedding. James just doesn't get it! A month or so ago, I caught James having sex on the internet. He said he'd only done it a time or two with just this one woman. He claimed it was no big deal. He says he wasn't really cheating on me, after all, he didn't really "do it."

Since then, I've done my homework and fired off a bundle of e-mails. James has been with over forty women in cyberspace and at least one of them was under age. The woman I caught him with says she really wants him.

Late last week I confronted him with what I knew. He made all sorts of promises to me, but within hours, he was back at the computer again. I told him he had to make up his mind—the reality of me and my two children or his fantasy woman. How do you fight fantasy?

- What are the issues for Rachelle and James in terms of their emotional, psychological, and relational health?
- What does Rachelle seem to expect from a faithful relationship? What does James assume? How might these differences be personified?
- Is fidelity negotiable in a committed and intimate relationship? How do Scripture and faith issues inform your answer? How does your own expe-

rience speak to this situation?
- How might fantasy threaten an intimate relationship?
- How do you counter fantasy in a real world?

Gayle

I'm adopted and an only child. My parents chose me. Why can't they just love me? We've always had this sort of "if . . . then" relationship — *if* I lived up to their current expectations, *then* they would love me.

The expectations were little when I was small—a perfect math paper, a memorized recital piece, or a passed swim test. As I grew older, the stakes got higher—talented and gifted programs, magnet schools, high grade point averages and standardized test scores, studying abroad. Occasionally I wouldn't measure up, the "calamity" would set-in, and I would be abandoned for awhile.

My college record with my parents was pretty good until the beginning of my senior year. That was the year that I broke my engagement with the son they never had and also decided that teaching wasn't the perfect career for me. I moved away from home after graduation. My folks caught up with my growing independence and eventually we all recovered from my college "setbacks."

A year ago last Christmas (just after my 25th birthday), I hosted my folks at my place. That's when I discovered the limits of our adult relationship. Two days after Christmas, I came out to my folks and told them that I am gay. They physically turned away from me, packed up their stuff, and within fifteen minutes (really!) walked right out of my life. We haven't talked or seen each other since.

If only I were "normal" and not a lesbian, *then* they could love me.

- Describe the promises of unconditional love from your own experience.
- How does parental acceptance fit into your expectations of unconditional love?
- How would you teach unconditional love to brand new, first-time parents?
- How might Gayle demonstrate the mutual love she craves?
- What might Gayle do in an attempt to restore this relationship?
- How is God in, with, under, and behind this family's actions?

SERVICE LEARNING OPTIONS

New faces, names, and circumstances can inform and nurture our love. To love is to do. Try one or more of these service learning options and act in love.

Idea #1: Call a Circle

Christina Baldwin, author of *Calling the Circle: The First and Future Culture*, offers a circle as a way to share leadership, give everyone voice, value different perspectives, and listen in a different way. A circle is a group of persons called together out of an urgent need or the desire to accomplish a definite task. Specific techniques are used to "hold" the circle. The circle works by consensus and spiritual guidance, practices discernment, and offers the support that its members want and need. Members of a circle agree to hold the circle, keep confidentiality, take responsibility, offer their own skills and abilities to think, listen to one another, and be led by the Spirit.

For more information, consult these resources:

- *Calling the Circle: The First and Future Culture*, by Christina Baldwin (Bantam Doubleday Dell, 1998).
- *The Millionth Circle: How to Change Ourselves and the World*, Dr. Jean Shinoda Bolen (Conari Press, 1999).
- Internet forum: *http://cafe.utne.com/millionthcircle*
- *Dance of the Spirit*, by Maria Harris (Bantam Doubleday Dell, 1991).

Idea #2: Advocate for Women's Economic Security

The story of Naomi, Ruth, and Boaz raises issues of women's security. Ruth and Naomi lived in a world in which women had to depend on male relatives to survive. Without a man, they had no legal or financial rights.

Recruit a cadre of bankers, financial advisors, and lawyers. Ask them to investigate private institutions and public policies regarding lending, ownership of property, and other questions related to the economic security of women. How does the legal and economic environment protect and empower single or displaced women? Invite these professionals to discern, decide, plan, and act in response to what they discover. Actions that advocate for the well-being of single women might include:

79

- equipping women to access legal and economic resources and services.
- providing assistance to recently widowed or newly displaced women.
- lobbying for new policies that facilitate economic independence.

Idea #3: Act on Behalf of Domestically Abused Women

Second Samuel accounts related acts of violence and abuse directed toward women. The experience of Bathsheba and Tamar continue to plague women today. Stand on the side of voiceless women like Bathsheba by refusing to give credence to efforts that attempt to:
- Scapegoat women (Bathesheba "asked for it").
- Rationalize arrogant misuse of power (David saved Bathesheba from mistreatment by Uriah).
- Romanticize the experience of women (David and Bathesheba were hopelessly in love).

Check local rape statistics and listen to anecdotal narratives. Compare what you learn with Tamar's experience. Were some or most women
- Assaulted by someone known to the victim? Raped in her own home?
- Exploited by her own kindness, hospitality, or upbringing?
- Saying "No," but were not heard and/or understood?
- Seeking help but told to be quiet?
- Seeking justice and restitution that was out of their hands?
- Diminished by public mourning over the perpetrator's grief or ruin?

Discern, decide, plan, and act in response. What might be offered to women like Tamar? (Men are also sexually assaulted; your efforts can certainly include working for justice and showing compassion for them as well.)

Idea #4: Establish a "Legacy of Love" Initiative

David pledged *hesed* to Jonathan and his household. Later, he acted in loving-kindness on behalf of Mephibosheth. David honored the legacy of love he shared with Jonathan.

The "Legacy of Love" concept is rooted in the expressions of loyalty and affection that others have offered on our behalf. Persons involved in the initiative would choose to act for the sake of others in ways that are similar to that of grandparents, parents, siblings, long-time friends, local church saints, and others who have loved them first. Such ministries of day-to-day compassion will honor and appreciate those persons who demonstrate love and create a legacy of neighbor caring. One-on-one mentoring programs and community-based agencies might benefit from a "Legacy of Care" initiative.